T0208098

Praise for *The Rival*

"Whether you're looking to improve a management style or inspire others, *The Rival* is an invaluable tool. No one can doubt the power of individuals to make a difference after reading *The Rival*. Whether you're in the catbird seat or you'd like to be, you'll benefit from reading *The Rival*'s seminal lessons about establishing successful global business relationships."

—Rick Kearns, Deutsche Telekom North America

"*The Rival* points the way to business success based on basic principles, including the ability to process information and establish behavioral change based on emotional intelligence. Readers will realize the importance of business strategy, group work, and having clear and pre-established goals. By following the guidelines in *The Rival*, you'll be able to turn a small idea into a powerful and competitive company."

—Edgar Pena, LMH, CAP

"Benjamin uses his experience to explain the key requirements to maximizing sales and creating a successful business. *The Rival*'s backdrop is Benjamin's success in the telecom industry, but its lessons can be applied to any business area. Benjamin's messages are artfully distilled and conveyed through real stories in a humorous, powerful, and engaging manner. Any sales professional or entrepreneur will find *The Rival* invaluable."

—Alan Geeves, partner, head of investment funds, N+1 Singer

"The same gift that first brought Benjamin to the attention of industry leaders is now the gift he shares with readers across the globe—insights about what makes great businesses, including branding, integrity, culture, clear vision, and philosophy. Readers of *The Rival* will leave with a clearer sense of purpose, drive, and renewed confidence in their business."

—Ilissa Miller, CEO, iMiller Public Relations, president, Northeast DAS + Small Cell Association

"Benjamin Von Seeger functions better than you do. That's just the way it is. You can lament the unfairness of this reality, or you can read *The Rival* and take advantage of his hard-won experience in building success at every level."

—John Kador, author of *The Manager's Book of Questions*

"*The Rival* is a guide for success. This practical book is rich with insight that will benefit both entrepreneurs and experienced businesspeople alike."

—Norma I. Salcido, director of marketing and communications, Guidance

"*The Rival*—a demystifying account of how, when, and why to conduct business in a competitive global setting. Benjamin Von Seeger introduces readers to his unique business strategies and tactics, which resulted in outstanding achievements and surpassed business stigmas and cultural boundaries. *The Rival* makes executives think outside the box in order to drive successful business realities."

—Gerardo Chaljub, PhD candidate, VP of human resources, main lecturer, and global consultant

"*The Rival* is must-read for students trying to bridge the gap between academics and practically. It follows the experiences of Benjamin Von Seeger, using modern-day theories to navigate the current trends in businesses and identify what works and what does not. *The Rival* provides key insights into building relationships, pursuing your passions, and achieving business success."

—Dr. Wayne M. Morgan, business professor

"I had the pleasure of working with Ben for many years. With *The Rival*, he has captured and shared the drive and passion for professional excellence that I witnessed every day. Balancing an international perspective with deep market knowledge, Ben brings a unique perspective to business. He has always understood that the foundation of long-term success is building lasting relationships."

—Jon A. DeLuca, former CEO of FiberNet Telecom Group, Inc.

"*The Rival* is the X factor revealed. Anyone wanting to solve the mystery of long-term success in sales and the art of deal closing should read and apply the techniques outlined in *The Rival*. While its instruction is practical, universal, and seemingly easy to execute, it is illusive to many who get locked into dead-end details. It's a textbook for what isn't textbook: integrity, talent, tenure, tenacity, and success."

—Betty Smith, CenturyLink

"Reading *The Rival* brought a smile to my face because it reminded me of the experiences Ben and I had together. *The Rival* is a great guidebook for the new generation of businessmen and women who want to lead the revenues of our newest companies being built. Succeeding in business is not just hard work; you have to have the right foundation. Each experience that Ben recites in *The Rival* is derived from his own successful foundation.

Having the right ethical behavior, as Ben highlights in *The Rival* time and time again, is what will allow you to last in the industry for as long as he has. The professionals that work alongside us in the industry and don't follow the gentlemen's code or have winning attitudes are never the leaders! My hope is that the individuals reading *The Rival*, listening to Ben's lectures, and those lucky enough to have been mentored by him follow a path to success that is paved with integrity and loyalty."

—Jamie Dos Santos, CEO of Cybraics and appointee to the President's Intelligence Advisory Board

"Benjamin Von Seeger portrays a rare hybrid of business development, sales, and execution skills in *The Rival*. *The Rival* is a great read for any entrepreneur who faces the challenges of hiring, retaining, or dismissing sales executives. Von Seeger goes beyond the initial contract signing to elaborate on what it really takes to understand complex buyers and generate revenue. Instead of introducing yet another sales gimmick, he focuses on core skills needed to drive sales and overcome the only real rival—yourself."

—Lionel Carrasco, founder and CEO, Leapfactor

"The past fifteen years helped me to learn and share Ben's core beliefs. *The Rival*, a book well worth reading, is the compilation of facts and effects of emotional intelligence that, combined, create the approach to successfully standing out in the competitive business environment."

—Marcela Henao, founder and CMO, Leapfactor

THE RIVAL

Play the Game,
Own the Hustle,
Power in Competition,
Longevity in Collaboration

Benjamin Von Seeger

OPEN BOOK
EDITIONS
A Berrett-Koehler Partner

iUniverse®

THE RIVAL

PLAY THE GAME, OWN THE HUSTLE, POWER IN COMPETITION, LONGEVITY IN COLLABORATION

To learn more or contact go to: www.benjaminvonseeger.com

iUniverse books may be ordered through booksellers or by contacting:

iUniverse
1663 Liberty Drive
Bloomington, IN 47403
www.iuniverse.com
1-800-Authors (1-800-288-4677)

Because of the dynamic nature of the Internet, any web addresses or links contained in this book may have changed since publication and may no longer be valid. The views expressed in this work are solely those of the author and do not necessarily reflect the views of the publisher, and the publisher hereby disclaims any responsibility for them.

Any people depicted in stock imagery provided by Thinkstock are models, and such images are being used for illustrative purposes only.
Certain stock imagery © Thinkstock.

ISBN: 978-1-4917-8081-7 (sc)
ISBN: 978-1-4917-8079-4 (hc)
ISBN: 978-1-4917-8080-0 (e)

Library of Congress Control Number: 2015918074

Print information available on the last page.

iUniverse rev. date: 03/08/2016

For my beloved father, Professor Dr. Gerhard Seeger, who taught me the most valuable lessons in life about relationships, languages, history, and respect for one another. Thank you, Father. I have become the man I am today because of you.

CONTENTS

PREFACE

Most businesspeople write books on their deathbeds to justify the way they've lived their lives. I understand this sentiment. At the end of a long and successful career, there is a desire to make sense of it. Looking back at all I've done, I find that it is not enough for me to just record it; I want to pass it on as a business tool for others. While this book is in part a recalling of a well-executed career, it is also a tool for those seeking to learn and follow in my footsteps. It's not just about being a good salesperson—it's about establishing and retaining a successful business.

People often ask me how I close deals. Suspecting my answer will sound too simplistic, I usually shrug off the question. It's not about being coy. There is wisdom in simplicity, so I will tell you it's all about relationships. Honestly, it's as simple as that.

What makes me an authority on global business, someone whose analysis and opinions are worthy of your attention? A track record of success.

Serving as a vice president at Terremark Worldwide Inc., NAP of the Americas, I secured multimillion-dollar contracts from national and international telecommunication carriers, content providers, and major corporations based in Latin America, Europe, Asia, and the United States. Terremark was a colocation and cloud-hosting provider that was sold to Verizon for $1.4 billion in 2011. Verizon paid $19 in cash for each Terremark share, about a 35 percent premium on the stock's closing price of $14.05 a share. A driver of innovation, I was also the director of global markets at CENX, the world's first carrier Ethernet exchange.

Results matter. In the end, they're all that matters.

While I'm an experienced business educator—I was visiting colecturer at DeVry University and its Keller Graduate School of Management, and I hold a degree in business administration and international relations from Ludwig Maximilian University of Munich—I'm also a lifelong student of business. I speak six languages, and at the moment, I'm committed to learning Portuguese. You have to commit to continuously growing and learning about your industry, because markets are always changing and evolving, very often overnight. That might mean learning about a new technology or studying a new language. If you don't make a commitment to your own success, you won't succeed.

About the Title: Departures and "A Rival"

In late October 2001, I was flying to London. It was a mere six weeks after the September 11 tragedy that shook the hearts of Americans and people all over the world. At that time, nobody was flying unless they absolutely had to. Security at airports was changing, and the air-travel business had a lot to lose from that senseless act of violence. I was sitting on a Boeing 777, which normally seats approximately 280 people. There were 43 of us on board, and that's including the crew. It didn't matter if I flew business class or coach; I could have run laps in the aisles with all the space on the plane.

People were being cautious about flying, and I couldn't blame them—but I was so used to traveling that jumping on a plane to tend to my usual meetings in London seemed like a no-brainer when I bought the ticket. Yet as I surveyed the empty aircraft, the wheels in my brain began to turn. An eerie fog of doubt crept over me. Should I consider modifying the way I did business? Could I change my method of pursuing contracts the way so many others obviously had?

The question hovered in the periphery of my mind. I was exhausted and jet-lagged by the time the plane landed. As I floated down the airport escalator, bags in hand, I could think of nothing else but checking into my hotel and checking one more box on my list of things to do. Above me hung a sign with the words "Departures" on one side and "A-rival" on the other. I did a double take, noting that "Arrivals" was spelled wrong. It took a moment for me to realize that it wasn't a sign but a billboard—or rather, a mock sign, posing as one of the directional signs I was so used to seeing all over the airport. Below the words "Departure" and "A-rival" was a witty tagline completing the advertisement: "If you're not going to see your customers, a-rival will." I chuckled to myself. Of course, if you didn't see your customers, a rival would swoop in and take what you left on the table.

Since that day in the London airport, the airways have once again repopulated with air traffic, and the world has grown in technologies that make meetings easier to arrange via teleconference. Just recently, someone asked me why I still fly. After all, we live in an age with Skype, FaceTime, and countless other ways to meet with someone without actually leaving your desk. The virtual meeting reigns supreme, or seemingly so. Here's why I default to face time instead of FaceTime.

On that trip to London, after I'd gathered my things and finally settled into my hotel, I ordered room service and began preparing my documents for the following day, leaving the TV on in the background. I heard a commercial for British Airways come on and casually turned my head to tune in. A salesman on screen was talking to a businessman via videoconference call. They were obviously in two different countries. The salesman spoke to his prospect, setting dates in the future when they would conference-call again, saying something like, "I'll look forward to speaking with you next week, and the week after, and the one after that as well."

They hung up, and the picture focused in on the prospect. The shot panned outward to show the prospect's office, then his desk, and finally a person sitting in front of his desk—another salesman. The prospect leaned over and signed a contract sitting in front of him, obviously issued by the salesman. The commercial ended there, fading to black with the British Airways logo hovering onscreen. A voice then repeated the tagline I'd read at the airport: "If you're not going to fly to see your customers, a-rival will."

I would love to meet someone else who remembers those ads as resolutely as I do, because they had such a profound impact on my life. So much so, in fact, that they have served as the inspiration for the logo design of my company, BVS Consulting Group, and the title of this book. The acronym stands for Benjamin Von Seeger; however, the check mark representing the letter *V* stands for much more than a part of my name. It represents the ability to get things done quickly and effectively to the best of my ability, with the notions that competition is ever present and there is always room to improve.

There I was, flying alone and even questioning why I was taking the time and energy out of my life to get in the same room as my customer, and here an airline was validating my experience. I do agree that virtual meetings have their place in the business world. In my book, however, they're only useful after you've made initial contact. Working on a deal can be tough enough—why cause relationship problems by allowing yourself to miss out on the additional benefits of human contact? Once you have secured the relationship and the deal, you can rely on videoconference calls and so on in lieu of constant travel. If you are an executive, get on a plane and establish a relationship. This is the work of making yourself real in the lives of your clients. Getting up and seeing people allows you to get to know the whole team, not just the champion.

A Message to Entrepreneurs

Why should young entrepreneurs eager to see their businesses rise to the top read this book? After all, there is a lot of information out there—especially on the Internet—about marketing, strategic business, branding, and how to build a successful company. I know because I've checked out the competition. Other authors profess to know the right way to lead a team, acquire accounts, and bring a business to the forefront of its industry. I'm not saying they're wrong. A lot of the information on the Internet is helpful.

The difference between those other authors and me, however, is simplicity. I am not interested in theory and hearsay; I am interested in fact and action. I meet young entrepreneurs every day, and what I've discovered is that there are two kinds: the kind who wear the title *entrepreneur* like a vanity necklace and the kind who see the life of an entrepreneur for what it really is—a hustle.

All negative connotations aside, being an entrepreneur means being a hustler. The truth is that many will get caught up in the ideology of the word *entrepreneur* and forget that the word really means "to take considerable initiative and risk; to lead others and participate in productive labor and business undertakings." A hustler is also an enterprising person who is determined to succeed. This person is a go-getter and pursues business with cunning and a limitless desire for success.

Don't get lost in the glory of the entrepreneur title. To commit to the hustle is to align yourself as the kind of businessperson who goes the distance. Everyone in the business world wants to be an entrepreneur, but how many are willing to sit in an airport for twenty-eight hours waiting for the perfect chance to speak to the person who will make their next big deal? The long hours, the tight schedules, the snap-judgment decisions—this is what builds a business. This is a hustle. If you are reading this book, it is to reinforce what you already know: the importance of working hard and taking major risks. The hustle, I learned at twenty-one, begins with sharp dress accompanied by a willingness and a strong commitment to serve confidently.

ACKNOWLEDGMENTS

I'd like to express my deep gratitude and sincere thanks to the people who saw me through the writing of this book, namely Philipp Seeger, Ana Serna, Edgar Pena, Crystal Cheatham, Joanna Styczen, and Saverio Guerriero. Without all of your help, support, hard work, and advice, this book would still be an amalgamation of ideas and thoughts inside my head. Thank you for making it a reality.

CHAPTER 1

The Key to Success

My first big break in business happened when I was twenty-one and matriculating out of school and into the workforce. Young, bright, and energetic, I worked as a service associate fetching cars for top businessmen. I'll never forget a man and CEO by the name of Frank Demmer who gave me my first big break. Frank continues to work in the industry today.

I managed a fleet of over five hundred cars for a communications company in Germany. The CEO always asked to have a specific Mercedes lined up for him when he went on business calls. I will never forget that car. It was a black Mercedes S500 with a navigation system. You're laughing because a navigation system is easy to come by these days, but it wasn't so common in 1994. Back then, a navigation system was like having the latest tablet today. I was the man he could count on to always provide him with that car and that utility. My ability to acquire those items on a consistent basis showed my initiative and willingness to follow through on projects assigned to me.

One day, as I handed the keys over to Frank, he started a conversation with me. He said, "Would you like to come work for me?"

His request seemed to come out of left field. Frank ran a technology company, and I was just a kid who was barely done with school. Couldn't he see that? Didn't he know I was just the man who ran the fleet for his company?

My problem was that I immediately proceeded to set up barriers and think of what I couldn't do. I put myself in the driver's seat of the situation and told myself I needed to shut this down, for both our sakes. I outright confessed that I knew nothing about technology. This was very true. At the time, I didn't even know how to use a cell phone. In those days, cell phones were new on the market, and it was a luxury to own one.

Frank is an incredible guy. He taught me a pivotal lesson that day that was later reinforced by months of training and years of working under him. I will never forget his response. He said, "It's not about the cell phone, it's not about technology, and it's not about how much you know or don't know. It's about relationships."

At that moment, he gained my attention. I was hired and thrown into a six-month boot camp for sales representatives with a hundred other people who were just like me. The caveat to being part of the class was the knowledge that it wasn't easy; we would either sink or swim. However, after I saw the first paycheck I earned and the prestige of being part of Frank's company and management team, there wasn't an ounce of failure left in me. I was determined to succeed no matter what. Clearly, not everyone shared my will and determination. When we graduated, there were only about twenty of us left. Among those twenty, I was at the top of the class.

When you are in a room that used to be packed and realize that you are one of the few still standing, it makes you think twice and hard. Many times I thought about the ones who weren't moving on with us. We were all given the same tasks to complete and tools to use. I was astounded at how many weren't able to keep up with the class assignments and ultimate requirements. Why was I still standing? Why had Frank chosen me and not the others employed within the car-service division?

Ultimately, it came down to consistency—with the cars as well as with the class assignments. In both situations, we were all given the same tools, yet I succeeded in providing the most consistent and efficient results. We were all taught the same things in class: how to talk to a customer, how to deliver boilerplate, how to make an offer, and how to close a deal. Learning the material mattered a lot. However, I was always at the top of my business because of how I applied the material and techniques thereafter.

There it was. I had to give Frank the credit because of what he had said to me. His wisdom ended up being so true and profound. It was about discernment. It was about being relatable. These were the elements of establishing relationships. All of the individual parts were coming together for me now. All I really needed was to commit to learning the technicalities of the business. Unlike the moment when Frank asked me to join his business, I now felt confident in my abilities. I was ready to get to work. After that, I worked for Frank for over six years, and my success only grew thereafter.

As proven by the failure rate of that boot camp, not everyone is driven and will succeed in the business world. It's just not possible because it is so competitive, and rightfully so. More importantly, schooling can teach you the book smarts of business and work experience will teach you street smarts, but your ability to assess a room, to speak to everyone as if you are addressing each person individually, is what gives you that competitive edge and confidence to close deals.

I saw this theory prove itself when I moved to the United States. I intended to sell my ideas to a female executive who was very high up in a technology company. I was so bold that I didn't even make an appointment to see her when I arrived in the country. I just walked into her office.

I had a reputation for putting a lot of effort into my overall appearance, and this day was no different. When I arrived, I looked smart and dressed for success. I approached the assistant's workstation with purpose and told her I had a meeting with her boss, Jamie. There wasn't a question about whether I belonged in the office or not. I'd already convinced myself of that. So, it is true that you mold and teach people how to treat you. Without hesitation, the assistant granted me permission to enter Jamie's office.

At that time, Jamie was building a new network access point, and it just so happened that I was selling fiber networks. Today, you can see that there is a natural marriage there, but back then, we were breaking ground and trailblazing this new business opportunity.

I remember walking into Jamie's office and saying, "I have an idea of how we can combine our two companies." I immediately had her attention, but I didn't stop there because I was on a mission. In the next couple of minutes, I began to lay out my intentions. I told her that with my contacts and her technology, we would sell our business products jointly.

To my surprise, I was in her office less than five minutes before she abruptly pulled the plug. "The meeting is over."

"Did I do something wrong?" I said to her.

"No, go speak to my assistant and we'll talk again next time."

I said to myself, *Damn, I messed up big time.* The meeting was only a few minutes, and now I was out on my behind. Worry and fear filled my heart, and I asked myself if I had really bungled the whole thing. And if so, which part didn't she like? I was frustrated that I couldn't read the situation. Knowing her after all these years, I am convinced that this was her way of testing her candidates' overall business acumen.

Regardless of how I felt, I waited to speak to the assistant. When I approached her workstation, she handed me an appointment card and to my disbelief stated, "You're having dinner with Jamie tonight at 8:00 p.m. at Morton's Steakhouse in Miami."

A few hours later, I was sitting in front of Jamie at the restaurant, where she shared some news with me. "I wanted to speak with you about something. I am going to be appointed as head of revenue of a new organization, and I need someone to run global sales. You are the guy to do it."

Later, she became the CEO. It was like déjà vu. Her offer had the same poise as Frank's six or so years before. "You don't even know me," I countered, not knowing what to believe. "You barely know my name, and you haven't seen my résumé or my work expertise."

Her response was just like Frank's. She said, "I don't want to see it. I don't care."

Six months after my initial dinner with Jamie and being engaged with her team, I closed her company's biggest deal for $6.8 million. I made it happen in a short time, and the deal came at a crucial moment, just when we needed to build our credibility in the market to increase our revenue stream. I later asked Jamie, "How did you know I was the one who could make it all happen?"

"You just know. Do you know how many hundreds of people walk into my office without getting my attention? You were in there five minutes and my attention was all yours."

In so many words, she was saying the same things that Frank said about forming relationships and having confidence to pique people's interest. When I walked into a room, I didn't go in with the charged bravado of ego. I went in with confidence and all the scruples of someone who is guided by a large amount of book smarts, street smarts, and most of all, emotional intelligence.

Let me reinforce and repeat that: above all, emotional intelligence is the key to success. It's not about having the most powerful handshake or getting heads to swivel in your direction when you enter the room; that stuff is all gravitas. I have discovered that confidence and self-assurance can go a long way. Clients can smell it, and they eat it up. Closing deals, however, is all about establishing business relationships. We will be examining emotional intelligence and the importance of relationships in greater detail later in the book.

CHAPTER 2

Creating a Global Corporate Environment

During my time as a visiting colecturer at DeVry University and its Keller Graduate School of Management, my students would often ask, "Why create a global company?" The answer is twofold: the Internet and the shrinking of the market. A starter company will strategically launch at a global level because selling products online increases customer sales globally and is cheaper than establishing a brick-and-mortar store. Entering the international market is the most efficient way to expand business potential.

So why should you take your established business global? Well, with the power of the Internet, your business is already global whether you realize it or not. The difference is how you choose to capitalize on your international customers' perception. You see, every business has eyes on it thanks to social media, the Internet, the need to increase market share, and the globalization of the entire economy.

Imagine you are a performer on a stage telling a stream of hilarious jokes to the crowd in front of you. As you speak and the audience responds with laughter, you come to realize that there is power in this performance. You know this audience well, and they become like putty in your hands. You know how to play them, and you do it well.

Now, imagine that your sixth sense is picking up something in your peripheral gaze. You turn to see that the curtain that once hung behind you has been lifted, revealing another audience. Some of them are chatting to themselves while others are giving you their rapt attention, demonstrating a strong interest. As a performer, you now have a choice: you have the opportunity to wield this power and duplicate your performance to both audiences, or leave it be and simply hope that the second audience grows to love you as much as the first.

This is a parable of the global economy set on the stage of the Internet. We now engage clients with ease, and sometimes without realizing that we are onstage and performing for customers who don't even speak our language or share our own culture and traditions.

As businesspeople, it is our job to turn around and face that new target audience. What I'm saying is that just because you're not aware of eyes focusing on you doesn't mean you're not being noticed. The beauty of it is that the power is all yours. You have the power to maintain brand integrity while tweaking your message to appeal to countries, cultures, and traditions to which you've never even been exposed. The key is to think outside the box and act as a global executive.

What Global Means and What It Takes

If anyone can do it simply by putting up a website, then going global means being strategic about the markets you enter. If international customers are engaging with your company for the first time by way of social media or your website, going global means creating a website that speaks directly to that audience. Your website will be accessible to eyes overseas. Use it to demonstrate brand agility by not only being live in other countries but also achieving a lasting presence in every major city around the world.

It will take time, strength, and fortitude to do this. However, the benefits far exceed the work involved. When I am asked by graduate students and business executives what it takes, I automatically hammer out this list:

- strong investors and business relationships
- global managers and teams who understand international and local business and cultures

- strategic business partners
- presence on the Web and integrated social-media strategies
- the assurance that the business can expand globally

I mention that last point because I want you to be aware that this market isn't for everyone. You can't take a pool-table company global the way you can take a phone company global. It's just not possible—unless the market for pool tables is extremely large and you are able to get pool-table stores in every major city. That's not the kind of work I'm talking about when I say to take your business global.

The Power of Language

Building successful business relationships is often easier when you and your prospects are speaking the same language. However, this often requires much more than just saying the same words.

You've decided that you want to make your website appeal to a global market, but once they have eyes on you, how do you ensure that you are conveying the right message and business strategy? What I've found with my business in the past and also today is that your message is a moldable fixture in this venture. The intent to assess this message is included in my planning for the next four months, with every market that I serve. The message from your organization has to be the same and must be culturally sensitive and appropriate from platform to platform.

When you approach these new markets, take a look at your brand in the context of that new country and do your market research. What do the people there spend their money on? What is the perception and culture like around your product? Who is your new audience, and what words would they want to see in your slogan?

When my students ask what they need in order to succeed in a global environment, my list is short and to the point:

- cultural competence
- ability to overcome language and traditional barriers

Spending adequate time on message is worth the effort it takes. It always comes down to word choices, and you will need to have your message translated to the common language and adjusted to the cultural context of the country.

Just think about all of the intricacies of language. If you've ever taken a language course, you know how difficult it can be to translate words and phrases into other tongues. Think of the minor differences between American English and British English. The same word in each country can mean something vastly different. We also use different words for the same items: Americans say French fries, the British say chips.

When translating from your native language, you will discover that it's not the literal words that change from country to country, it's the connotation of the words. A connotation can cloud the meaning of the word and derail your message and business prospects. Those who know both the language and the culture will be savvy in their ability to translate your message to that specific market. They will convey the context as well as the literal meaning. A great example of this is Spanish, the most spoken language in the world after English.

You must master a language and culture in order to achieve a uniform feel in the market you are prospecting. I love languages and had to learn them out of necessity in order to master different cultures and business markets. I am currently proficient in six languages, but I realize that this is not possible for most busy chief executive officers.

I don't expect every CEO to speak six languages. However, I do expect all CEOs to hire the right talent who can offer culturally sensitive insight and even translate for them when the time is appropriate. Like I said earlier, each businessperson must know his or her personal bandwidth as well as individual strengths and weaknesses. It is a credit to the company when individuals do this and assimilate themselves within a global environment.

My native language is German, but I have people in place who can translate the minute connotations of language when I am in Brazil, Spain, France, or any corner of the world. To avoid brand failure due to cultural ignorance, find someone who can clearly articulate what your brand says in any country. Tell that person what you want your brand to project and sound like, and then follow the advice when he or she suggests which words to use. Consideration needs to be given to the colloquialisms of the country in question. The translation of the brand is the most important element to success.

CHAPTER 3

Developing a Brand

There are millions of companies in the world competing for a piece of the pie. A solid brand identity can be the key to making sure your business stands out from the crowd. Developing an effective brand sets the foundation for all other components. From logo creation to color selection to content development, there are several different pieces to creating a perfect brand that we'll discuss in this chapter.

Branding and Marketing: the Chicken or the Egg?

Adapting that old saying, I'll ask which came first: the marketing or the branding? Some would say the marketing, and others would say the branding. I like to think outside the box and say neither applies to all situations. If you ask me, finding the true value comes before marketing and branding. After you've discovered the value of your business, you should have a very clear idea of what your market is and what your brand is telling customers. You must have solid customer care and quality in any brand in order to be successful.

It's a tricky question, because there are moving variables in a brand just as there are moving variables in a market. If you can keep your eye on the value of your company, you can manage all of the moving pieces and ultimately solve the puzzle.

Naming Your Business and Creating a Logo

When I decided to branch off into global consulting, I set out to select a name for my company that was strong and could stand the test of time. I chose BVS Consulting because I needed the name to be recognizable across borders. Those are my initials and the cornerstone of my brand, capturing my business savvy. I gave the company a title my clients and contacts would be familiar with.

People I'd built relationships with over the past eighteen years knew my name and knew my work. In essence, I was the value of the brand. Therefore, I didn't want to risk diluting the value of my business by asking clients to remember a new name for my brand. After all, they had a relationship with me. Simply put, brands are relationships.

You can do the same thing whether you are starting a brand from scratch or building on an old business idea. When naming your business, you will want to follow the logic that you are maintaining an ongoing relationship with your customers. Create a name that is familiar to your target audience. If you are starting from scratch and want to distinguish yourself from the competition, make sure that your brand name is easy to identify and lets people know what business you are in. Remember, if it's too ambiguous or wordy, you risk being lost in the shuffle of competitors.

After naming the business, I needed a logo. Logos can be tricky because ultimately, you want something that is both trendy and attractive. However, something that is trendy and attractive today may not be tomorrow. It also must make business sense. Just take a look at the fashion industry. Every season, there is a new way to wear a shirt, pants, and shoes. Style is always shifting because humans are constantly evolving in taste. Or consider AT&T. In the 1990s, the color blue was very popular in branding. At that time, AT&T, IBM, and many other businesses were sporting blue-and-white logos. Today, orange is the new blue.

We could also take a long look at font. In the 1990s, it was common to see serif fonts. Serif refers to the small projecting features on gothic-style fonts. Times New Roman is a perfect example. Today, sans serif fonts (fonts without projecting features) are the most popular and acceptable because they are easier to read and work better on websites.

Companies like AT&T and IBM achieved success by maintaining brand recognition while reworking their logos to incorporate popular trends. There is nothing more important than being flexible and adaptable in the business world—especially when change forces your business to implement new ways of operating and adhering to new market trends. Flexibility is achieved when a business is able to keep a firm grasp on core values while discerning the market.

Ultimately, your logo should reflect your message to the market. Just be careful: changing a logo too many times can be perceived as organizational instability. The key is to consult with your target audience before introducing a change of logo. Consider the Gap logo change, which led to a confused customer base, rapid decrease in sales revenue, and, ultimately, major changes in the corporation's executive management structure. Bottom line: it may not always be beneficial to fix things that aren't broken.

Enhancing Your Message with Colors and Images

There are several questions I needed to ask myself when establishing my brand and message. For instance, I wanted people to know that I had cloud, fiber-optic, and data-center solutions. My message to the world had to be recognizable upon first encounter. Sitting and thinking about what message I was sending also helped me in creating my logo.

The first question I asked myself was, "What are your customer demographics?" Knowing your customer base will help you identify your purpose and value in the market. For instance, there is a big difference between a message that appeals to parents and a message that appeals to teenagers. Parents are a demographic that wants affordable services that go a long way; teenagers are a demographic that wants what is cool or popular and needs the service to be inexpensive. If you look at the way Apple sells iPhones to parents and teenagers, you'll notice that their message changes from one demographic to the next.

My second question was, "What is your customer perception?" In other words, I needed to know how my customers viewed my company and what they were expecting me to deliver. My clients knew me as the guy who got things done and delivered a certain standard of excellence. It was imperative that my brand send this same message across borders. If there was a task on a list left incomplete, I was the guy hired to make sure that the ultimate task was checked off and delivered in a timely fashion. With BVS Consulting, I wanted to reflect the same attitude of preparedness and execution. What says, "We offer assured acceleration and growth for your company"? Orange accentuates energy and effectiveness. That is how I chose the orange checkmark for my logo. I needed my message to get across, and so far, the logo is doing its job extremely well.

The third question I asked myself was, "Who are you trusting to create your message?" I want you to think long and hard about this because it is important to know your limits. I'm an executive—I do what I am good at, and that's why I'm successful. Knowing your bandwidth as a company is just as important as knowing your limits as an individual.

Let me give you an example. I was the one calling the shots when my website initially went live. I made many of the decisions for the designers, and in the end, the website was subpar. I am an idea man and can offer some great advice, but in that situation, I really needed to trust people who create branding and key messages for a living. It was in my best interest to hire a new design firm as well as a public-relations team by the name of iMiller Public Relations to reformat and rewrite my website. Both companies were able to refine my message and website design to ensure both were clear and spoke directly to my target audience. Most importantly, they ensured that my business model was communicated in an easy and efficient way.

Content That Makes an Emotional Connection

When in the creation stage of your brand, there are things you should ask yourself when trying to give your brand personality. Whether the personality comes from the brand or the individual product, it is imperative that you make yourself aware of what your message is to the world. Just as it is important to be aware of yourself in a room full of strangers, it is important to be aware of what you are saying to the world through your brand or product. You can start by asking: Who? Why? And how?

- The **who** is the demographic your product appeals to. Think of car commercials during the Super Bowl. Each luxury car is still a luxury vehicle, but the manufacturer will choose a different word to represent it. That is because each of those words represents a different demographic of people. If Mercedes-Benz knows that accomplished academics are the people who generally buy their vehicles, they are going to use words that accomplished academics gravitate toward or use themselves. *Prestige* is one of those words.
- **Why** are you interested in focusing on that angle? What is the value for the customer and what is the value for you? Unless you are empathizing with the customer and really know what it is the customer expects and wants, you may just be chasing your own tail.
- **How** does it compare to other products of its kind? This is important to establish, because you want to know who is doing what you are doing. Are they doing it better? What makes you better than them? By observing your rival, you will discover where you stand to cultivate the most growth.

Products, like people, have personalities, and personalities evoke emotional responses. It is in your best interest to create the kind of personality in your product that will evoke the right kind of emotions from your demographic. The personality of your product can be established by envisioning what the demographic believes about the product. When you affirm beliefs through motion, color, typography, and composition, global customers will share in the ideas your product puts forth.

My friend Michael Estrada taught me a very important lesson about the way you can create a personality for your product. He believes that a product must be agreeable to the customer, sparking an emotional response. After all, facts don't interest people; art and story are what make a product likable. In his talks, Estrada shares a lot about the emotional connections people have and how this connection trumps expense. People care more about how a product makes them feel than how much it ends up costing.

I want to talk a bit about this because I've witnessed just how truly smart this reasoning is. Emotional connections are what keep customers coming back long after they've tried and liked your product. Salespeople who work in advertising need to understand that they sell the end product of their customer, not advertising.

Global Branding: A Case Study

In the past, I represented a Mexican telecommunications organization that had a presence in twenty-six different countries within eleven years of its launch. Their website was translated into three languages, and the company represented five different brands. I have to give recognition to an organization that was able to propel a product to market worldwide with such a far-reaching grasp. Unfortunately, they were failing to keep their brand recognition intact and cohesive. This flaw was eroding their profits because of weakened brand strength and nonexistent customer recognition.

When I set foot in the company office, I noted that its failure was not due to common pitfalls, such as poor customer service, shoddy product support, or low-quality phones. It wasn't primarily due to the company's lack of competence; it was purely a matter of customer perception. People didn't recognize the company from country to country. It was as if they'd started with a great product in Guatemala and then recreated their model in every new country. Management style and customer perception are not universal.

The organization launched twenty-six different websites with the exact same number of messages, designs, and approaches. The CEO approached me and asked, "Ben, tell me sincerely what I am doing wrong. We are not getting the brand recognition that we need in order to reach our company goals." I was not surprised to hear that their approach was not working. There was no consistency in brand or messaging. But I had a solution.

The CEO wanted my absolute honesty, so of course, the gloves came off. In a conference room, we pulled up all of the branding information from twenty-six different countries—colors, messages, websites, and all. "In my opinion," I said, "it looks like Cirque du Soleil. I don't know what you're doing, much less what you are selling or the message that you are trying to convey. If this scattered message is what goes out to your customers, then it's also being reproduced internally. It's failing all target audiences."

I told that CEO the same thing I will tell you: the message was destroyed in the distraction of having twenty-six different websites. First of all, the palette of colors needed to change and offer one uniform presentation across all borders. Second, they needed to hire stellar translators so that the original message permeated the brand image and became uniform in every single country served. The marketing, storefronts, and especially the company name had to be consistent across all internal branding amongst employees and business units, as well as external branding for the consumer. Whether it was England, Spain, Portugal, or another country, the company brand and message needed to be recognizable from one airport to the next.

Think about McDonald's. Everywhere you go in America, their French fries taste exactly the same. You can even travel to South Africa, South America, or Europe, and those McDonald's French fries taste like you picked them up around the corner from your house in the United States. What does this do for a company's brand? It sends a clear message internally as well as to the consumer that your services are unwavering and consistent across all markets.

Next, I set to work ironing out the discrepancies between the company's websites and internal branding and messaging. Changing the mentality and approachability in twenty-six countries was time-intensive and certainly no easy task. Consumers also needed time to adapt to a new look. Nevertheless, internally, the company was growing into its new uniform shoes. It took me two years to work out all the kinks, but today, you can go to the company's website and see great changes and innovative brand identification. There is a list of countries on the main page, and each of those web pages is uniform. In an effort to bridge the language barrier, visitors have the option of translating the page into their native language.

In the time this has taken, the organization has learned how not to overwhelm the customer with pictures and information, and also the key to using stock photos, which can be edited in Photoshop or another design program so that the pictures are personalized to your page and marketing standards. It is true what they say: less is more, and it gets the message across more effectively.

CHAPTER 4

Know and Love Your Business

Marketing and branding are the sizzle of a company. They are the cherry on top of your masterpiece, but the whole confection will surely fall flat if it has no substance to it.

Have you ever watched the television show *Shark Tank* on ABC? It's okay if you haven't. Most of us don't have time to watch television, and if we do, it's because we are on vacation. I want to talk about *Shark Tank* because there is something unique that happens during the vetting process for each new business. The scenario lines up four investors, all of whom made their money by building businesses from the ground up. These people have done remarkable work in their fields, and each brings a unique understanding of his or her respective market to the show. During the show, four to five people take turns trying to wow these investors, known as sharks, with their business idea in order to receive an investment.

The business owners who find themselves on this show have created and grown their businesses into fairly successful ventures. Each of them is vetted by the sharks, one at a time. The sharks want to know what their profit margins are, how much they made in the past year, who their suppliers are, and if they are working out of their basements or renting out retail space.

It's a cutthroat interview. If the business owners do not reply with a believable or viable answer, the sharks eliminate them. If their margins are too small, they are also out. If the business isn't mature enough for an investor to jump in, then the deal is off. I've seen so many bowed heads walk out of that door without receiving funding because the person didn't think through the answers properly before speaking and communicating a convincing pitch.

The worst scenario, though, is to see a business owner walk into the presence of those investors, bat every question out of the park, and still not secure a deal. Wouldn't you kick yourself if you got that far and choked? I watched an episode featuring a doctor who sparred with the sharks about his invention. The doctor was already making a large amount of money, but in order to make his idea succeed, he needed to put in a lot more time. He needed to believe in his product enough to walk away from his current position. He came to the sharks expecting them to invest so that he could hire someone to do the footwork. He wanted to keep his job because it was safe, but he also wanted to keep building his business because it was his dream.

When a business is getting off the ground, nobody sells a product like the founder. Nobody will make the passionate, cutthroat decisions like the creator, and no one will go the distance and do whatever it takes unless it is his or her brainchild. In this situation, the sharks got all the way up to the last hurdle and decided not to invest in the man's business. I was impressed by their decision, because this matched my own belief and business experience.

If you are building something, you have to be willing to jump into the deep water when the time comes. It will be hard work, of course. You will probably feel insecure about many of your decisions, but the reward will be worth it. When you jump in and commit to doing your work, you will learn things about your business that not a single textbook can teach you. I'm a firm believer in the school of life. As businesspeople, we can't always stay clean. Sometimes, we have to jump in and get a little dirty while closing a deal. It is survival of the fittest.

My advice to you is *know your business*. Learn the numbers and know the answers to the hard questions. Work until all sounds of distraction fade away, and it is just you and your envisioned goal that remain. Just as an athlete must train rigorously before performance day, you must create an ideal concept and environment in which your business can succeed. "Get in the zone," as some would say.

Fine tune, get close, listen in, and get to know the nervous system of your business. You are the one who created it, who brought it to life, and you have to be the doctor who keeps it alive. You are a scientist, and this is your research project. As such, you know its ins and outs and ups and downs. Get into it and make it your all-consuming passion. Those who are not obsessed with their businesses ultimately fail. Don't let that happen to you.

Clear Vision and Mission Strategy

Vision and mission drive strategy. Clear vision and mission occur when you take the time to set and commit to goals. Take a look at your company. What do you want to accomplish? Put that at the very top of your goal list as your finish line and work backward, building a strategy to accomplish it. Understand that you will hack away at achieving your goals on a daily basis. Some days you will succeed and others you will fail. When you fail, it is your prerogative to go back to the drawing board and correct your flight pattern. Get it right and then get back out there. Get comfortable being uncomfortable.

I had an experience that I want to tell you about. I think it will help you see how important it is to wake up with a clear vision of your job for the day.

I'm not always the boss—you may not believe this, but I actually have personal time, and in that time, I have hobbies. I am an athlete and spend a lot of time keeping my heart healthy. I go on trips, dine out, and enjoy the company of friends and family. In each of these situations, I am most likely someone's customer. At the gym, I am a member and benefit from the commitment to customer satisfaction. When traveling, I expect my airline to get me to my destination safely and in a timely manner. In a restaurant, I am a patron. You get the gist. If in any of these services promised are not rendered, I, as the customer/patron/member, can become frustrated.

Some time ago, I decided that I would consult a Realtor in order to buy some property. I knew what I wanted to spend and was looking at condos in the $475,000 price range. One day, I got a call from my Realtor, who said, "Ben, come meet me at this location." So I dropped what I was doing, got myself to the location, and met the Realtor who then proceeded to show me the condo.

There I was, a person with the intent to buy. The condo was a product on a shelf, and I am not someone who needs to be convinced that I want the product. I am also not someone who needs to be convinced that I can afford the product. I am everyone's favorite customer. I am the guy who only needs to be convinced that the item is to my liking. At that moment, it was my Realtor's job to convince me that I liked the condo. This is not what happened.

I began to ask my Realtor questions about the space. Simple things like, how much square footage? What are the association fees and how often must I pay them? How about the amenities of the building? How many extra parking spots could I buy?

Rather than responses, I heard hesitation and stumbling with every question. She would often shrug and say, "I'll get back to you with more information on that." What a dreary response to give someone who came into the corral rearing and ready to go. I was a bull, and she was treating my time and energy like we were playing, like it was some kind of dance. I can tell you for sure that she didn't wake up that morning with the intent of selling me a condo. I walked out of there empty-handed, with too many unanswered questions. Truly a lack of thoroughness and preparedness for someone who was ready to close a deal.

Not many customers will return to an item or service—or condo for that matter—after having a negative experience with a salesperson. They will brand and rate the company by their poor experience and proceed to bad-mouth it whenever the name comes up.

In this case, I was very interested in what I saw of the condo. I called the real estate company and asked for another representative. Again, I got a call from a real estate agent. He told me to arrive at the building, and I arrived expecting answers to my questions. I was, after all, a buyer with an open checkbook.

The new agent was overflowing with information about the condo. I didn't know anyone could pack so many items of discovery into a description of a bathroom, molding, or even the kind of tile that was laid in the kitchen. Where I saw wood floors, he saw imported bamboo. I had questions, and he had answers on top of answers. I quickly grew overwhelmed by what he had to offer. The best part, though, was that he showed up with a contract. This is the way to make a customer's head spin.

I would like to think that this real estate agent woke up with a strategy. He had the intent of selling me that condo, and he wasn't going to give me an opportunity to walk away without it. I don't know how many condos he memorized the architectural layouts for, but I was glad he did it for mine. He came into the opportunity with a clear focus on what he was going to do, and he walked toward his goal as if the difference between achieving it and not achieving it was showing up. As the customer, I felt taken care of. I felt that he respected my time. I was so impressed that I pulled out my checkbook and said, "How much?" I was ready to buy.

You see, customers, like investors, don't have time. They want a suited professional to give them direct, polished answers. If you are a customer, you want these things. When I am a customer, I want these things. After all, I trust each business with my very valuable, very expensive time, and probably my contacts to boot.

Let's take a moment to compare the two Realtors. The first was comfortable and had decided that approaching the sales floor with caution was her best strategy. The second put himself through a grueling study session, learned everything there was to know about the condo, and then wowed me with his knowledge and overwhelming sales pitch. The difference that I noted in these two situations is the expectancy of being comfortable.

At any stage of the game, if you're comfortable, you're not doing it right. Always be agile in preparation. Don't lose confidence in your meetings, because customers will sense it right away. Their body language will falter, and then the meeting is over. If you have the knowledge in your back pocket, you can step in with confidence. Knowledge is power, and the devil is in the details. Know your details and act upon them confidently.

Adapt or Die

Humans are afraid of change—we are terrified of it. We like predictability and stability, but that is not the way the world works. If you are a new company getting your bearings straight in an ever-shifting market, your dictum should be to obey change and submit by adjusting your course. Change is inevitable, but its course requires great adaptability and acceptance at every angle.

With my *Shark Tank* example, I tried to illustrate how important it is to jump into your work headfirst without hiring someone to do it for you. Eventually, as your company grows, you will need to hire people. The final frontier is that moment when you lean back in your seat, tug the wheel toward your chest, and start to lift off. In this moment, you are not riding on your own manpower. By this time, you are working with so many designers, salespeople, platforms, and teams that the only way to stay airborne is to pull in more hands to complete the ever-growing task list.

After hiring all of these people and expending all of your resources, the final straw will be to pick your sales leader. Successful sales executives must be able to do the following:

- handle challenging new situations while thinking on their feet
- work through their project team to meet goals and deadlines
- motivate team members and create a work plan
- assume responsibility for each step of a project
- unfreeze, change, and refreeze when introducing a change-climate environment

Your team is so important during the first twelve months of your business because how you drive and conduct business will change constantly. When I worked with Terremark Worldwide, I knew that I would be reshaping the company over the first twelve months. I shared my vision with my sales executive, who then relayed that message on to the team. What mattered to us was the life of the company.

We paid close attention to customers and to which direction the market was flowing. It was always shifting and changing under us. In turn, we also shifted and changed. While we were highly responsive to market needs, we did our best to balance that with innovation in order to remain profitable. It was the only way to survive in a difficult marketplace: change, adapt, or die.

I remember some of the grueling work we did in those first three months. We hired twenty sales reps and quickly got to work. At the end of a few months, we noted that we weren't performing our best. Our numbers showed that we had customer interest, but we weren't following through with great sales results. Customers were coming to us with open checkbooks, and we were selling them product at an alarmingly low rate.

What did I do with my sales director? I told her to fix it. We went through each salesperson's files and discovered which individuals had adjusted to the incredibly steep curve we'd supplied them. Our analytics showed that only about four of them were continuously getting great results, while the others were acting as dead weight.

Some will ask why we didn't take the time to train them on how we wanted them to sell efficiently, but at three months in, we didn't have the data to teach them anything. We needed people with skill and the ability to execute.

We fired the sixteen low performers, gave the remaining four their accounts, and went back to the drawing board to hire more sales reps. During the first twelve months, we had a high turnover, but we didn't let it affect us, because we weren't trying to be babysitters. We were so focused on our goal that even the competition faded into the gray haze. We focused on our customers, we focused on our market, and before we knew it, we were playing ball with major competitors—and we were enjoying both short- and long-term wins.

Focus to Win

With all of the flying around and working endless hours, it can be easy to lose focus. At the end of the day, I'm not flying around to rack up frequent-flyer miles. My goal is always to seal the deal, to achieve the contract. I'll be the first to admit that coming to agreement over the terms of a working arrangement is not easy. Each contract is not a cookie-cutter mold of the next. My life would have been much easier if each new acquisition wanted the same thing as the last.

As a global salesman, I decided to meet each of these challenges with a positive attitude and a mission to be innovative and different from the next. You have to be creative when making deals. There's no way around it. That is where the real alchemy in building a business comes from. It's a conflation of relationship building, emotional intelligence, and knowledge of what your company can and cannot do. It also requires a lot of patience and willingness to perform as the brains of the operation.

Each customer has wants, needs, and desires. These wants will appear to you as barriers, however unintentional they may be. These wants and needs can make the contract stage go on for a long time, but it is your job to follow through with the process.

I remember I once had a request for proposal (RFP) with IBM that took ten months to respond to. It required several meetings with their team, and I had to coordinate my teams in order to effectively respond to the RFP. Some of the business transactions we have in our lives are going to be very complex. We have to be able to come up with a way to bridge the gap between what the customer wants and what we are able to deliver.

The negotiations aspect of securing a deal can be complex and time-consuming. There are ways to give yourself a boost though. Some people see the chasm between their organization and what the customer wants, and without the tools of creativity and innovation, they stop short and never reach the end of the deal. It can happen to anyone. It's always smart to ask for help. There's nothing wrong with not knowing everything, so talk to your peers and gain that extra push to move you forward.

Another way to make sure that you are crossing your t's and dotting your i's is to pursue constant customer feedback. Ask customers questions about their budgets and what they were comfortable with. It is best to come back with a clear number instead of a ballpark, so I worked with my customers, asking questions in order to achieve that. After meetings, I basically surveyed the customers verbally, taking note to remember their reflections. I asked customers for their thoughts on our team's delivery, legal agreement, contract presentation, delivery time, and all kinds of other things. I'd rather hear from them than fumble the whole play once the contract is signed. I made an effort to change things they weren't happy with as quickly as possible. The key was that I could take constructive criticism and adapt, and then come back and do it better.

Apple and Amazon did it backward. They started working with group and feedback studies. Once they'd gathered enough information, they went and built the businesses they knew the public desired. There's nothing wrong with asking for feedback from the very first meeting. Square that away up front and then deliver it. Even this book was built on questions from my graduate students.

CHAPTER 5

A Brief Reflection on Strategy

Having a clear direction and strategy are critical aspects of any successful business. I once had a meeting with a company that had a great position in the market. Originally, they sought me out as a global consultant and eventually wanted to incorporate my company, BVS Consulting, into their work. I was very excited about this and immediately started to look into their organization and business model.

On the surface, they were booming. The company was leagues above its competition, and I knew that with my consulting, they could get even more business. Yet as I did my due diligence, I came across information that I wasn't thrilled about. Not everything that shines should be perceived as gold.

Once I had a look at their business strategy, or lack thereof, I realized we had a problem. The CEO was running a very chaotic ship. For example, the roles of leadership in the company were not well defined. They didn't have the right people working for them, and it was apparent that they were wasting crucial business resources and seeking out the answers to problems in roundabout and inefficient ways. They were running on luck, and I cringed for the day their luck would run out and I'd be forced to try to save an already sinking ship.

When it came to my role in the company, the CEO had a disjointed view of how I could serve. He saw me as an agent, not as a global executive who had the company's best interest at heart. Why he saw me as an agent had nothing to do with my performance; it had everything to do with his lack of business strategy, focus, vision, mission, and organization. From that angle, it was impossible for him to see how he could integrate my company within his business. I went into the relationship thinking I would get a big contract with them, but ultimately, I had to walk away considering his lack of vision. Walking away wasn't a blow to my ego, however. Rather, it illustrated how well I knew myself, my business, and my expectations.

It will be in your best interest as a young entrepreneur to know when you should stick it out with an offer and when you should walk away from something that will tear apart the integrity of the company you've built. This is what I enjoy about having my own business: by executing my own strategy, I have the luxury of refusing business that isn't going to enhance my operations. As a global consultant, I could have brought this business organization to its ultimate height and received a paycheck on the back end, but I walked away because I have a standard for my business.

My long-term objective is to work with global companies that have long-term goals as well as the seasoned business acumen to succeed. A company that through simple, shallow observation doesn't have itself together is not going to further the legacy of any brand. Moreover, it's not something with which I want to be associated. I looked at that company and predicted failure in the near future. This could have been prevented by a simple business strategy, focus, clear vision, mission, and organization.

In contrast, while working with Terremark, I was clear for the first twenty-four months on what steps and direction to take:

1. Create critical mass and bring every single major carrier to my data-center facility.
2. Develop and sell a space to demonstrate to investors that I am successful in my business.
3. Create managed security services and later cloud services, and manage them across the board.

I wrote these down and posted them on my door. I had a very clear strategy for the business, and that's why I systematically became successful.

So, when it came to working with this new business endeavor, I saw these fault lines and took the observation back to my board of directors. They recognized and shared my thoughts. I was directed not to move forward with the deal. Being business savvy and recognizing potential failure is a key factor when prospecting for business deals.

I don't care what kind of business you have, if you don't have short- and long-term goals, you may not get to your end result. This makes you realize that it looks good on the outside, but the inside is an abominable mess. How will you go forward with a clear direction? How will you grow your business and market base? You won't. You will spend the second stage of growth untangling a mess that could have been avoided in the first place. Key consideration needs to be given to proactive strategies rather than reactive strategies.

CHAPTER 6

Corporate Culture: On Trust, Team Building, and Integrity

Any company that puts greed and self-enrichment before its customers and shareholders is ruining the marketplace for all other corporations. A few years ago, I was listening to an NPR story, "Trust In America: Recovering What's Lost," that spoke of the overall mistrust Americans have of their government and, in turn, of the giant corporations that seemingly control all of the money that filters in and out of it. The story aired when opinions about the government were low, the market wasn't doing well, and a growing mistrust and dislike of the "1 percent" was beginning to materialize. The Occupy Wall Street movement was also on the rise, and everyone's thoughts were on companies that said one thing and did another with their constituents' monies.

The research-based global performance-management consulting company Gallup surveyed national trust among Americans over a sixty-year period. The study showed that four out of five Americans trusted government and businesses in the 1950s. With every recession, that number has fallen a little more. In 2015, the public relations firm Edelman reported in its Trust Barometer report that trust levels in business decreased in sixteen of twenty-seven countries and now sits below 50 percent. What we are learning is that people simply don't trust the organizations that they leverage and, in many cases, even work for.

As I read this news, my thoughts were focused on corporate culture and the shortcomings that lead to public displays of illegal activity, fraud, and insider trading. These are extremes, but it is the acceptance of deceit and a willingness to overlook integrity that gets a company to commit such egregious crimes. Collectively, it is a consequence of greed that we in the corporate world are all turning up losing hands. The market was built on trust. If we don't have that anymore, what are we left with?

Do you remember Enron? The 2001 scandal and prompt collapse of the corporation triggered a colossal turn in the market. Once the seventh-largest company in America, Enron was bankrupt in mere months. When its facade fell, the entire American public saw that the company's parade of revenue was nothing but smoke and mirrors. Its employees lost thousands of jobs and the organization lost the respect of a nation.

Enron was one of the companies listed in the aforementioned 2011 NPR special and just one of many that corroded the customer/corporation trust relationship. I shake my head just thinking about it now, because I think those CEOs were getting away with a lot, right under the public eye. People look at that and think, "If they could do it once, who's to say that other companies aren't doing it now?"

What can I say? It is "our" fault. The moral of this story is that as a result of this corruption, many regulations and guidelines were instituted to protect the interest of employees and stakeholders. Over my fifteen-year career, I've dealt with people who created companies and legacies. They were trailblazers and heroes of their time, but not all of them created corporate roads and inlets with a clear conscience. In my work, I've come across too many people who have had a clearly negative impact on corporate culture and the business environment.

Not surprisingly, I was disgusted by Enron's attitude toward off-the-books accounting. Yes, the company's approach to hiding losses, inflation, and unregulated private partnerships eventually took them down, but it hurt all of us—and, most importantly, public interest—in the process. Unfortunately, we are all in this polluted bath together. And the story continues today with many other business interests at stake.

Why spend so much time talking about trust and integrity, especially in the corporate world? After all, trust and integrity speak to virtue and morality. Do these words belong in business vernacular?

Yes, I say they do, and here's why. Trust is more than a social virtue; it is the currency of the global economy. When people trust your company, they value your company, and it generates consensus across the board. All you really have between the pomp and circumstance of public relations and marketing is value. You need your customers to value you as much as your employees and investors; otherwise, you are nothing but a gimmick destined to achieve failure and unsuccessful outcomes. Trust is the lubrication of both the capitalist machine and the global market. Without trust, nothing moves as it once did.

What I'm trying to get at is that when people don't trust corporations, they hang on to their dollars, affecting our economies of scale and leading to stagnant supply and demand. So now, we are fighting against the inefficiency of mistrust, and that makes our job even harder because we must prove ourselves. We used to be given the benefit of the doubt. Now, gaining the trust of a customer proves to be much more difficult. It becomes a major undertaking to achieve customer trust; we need a long-term vision where increasing market share is key

Trust in the Office

The trust of customers isn't the only thing businesses need to worry about. To avoid costly employee turnover, it is important to instill a culture of trust in your office. If your team doesn't trust you, they will be working for political gain and looking for better jobs as soon as it makes sense for them logistically. The rehiring process can cost you a great deal, which is why you should work to retain employees as much as possible.

I've found that training is a great way to instill a positive group dynamic, one where people feel confident in their strengths and are willing to ask for help when they need it. Training and development are crucial investments for ongoing success. Lack of these important initiatives results in a stagnant organization with virtually no drive or motivation. These short- and long-term investments need to be preserved and maintained in order for companies to retain their best talent. Turnover introduces failure to this type of investment.

I'm saddened when I approach the corporate world. I sometimes have to shake my head in disbelief. This is part of the reason why I left it behind to start my own global consulting firm. When living the corporate life at the CEO and executive-team levels, it is easy to get caught up in the extravagance of what you're doing. In that zero-gravity environment, you start to believe that you have superhuman powers, that you are untouchable. This is only true if you are neglecting the system of checks and balances put into place to regulate decisions made at that highest level in order to align business objectives and your market demands.

The behavior of corporate leadership at companies like Enron is both disgusting and somewhat sociopathic. It's not healthy for an individual to think and live like that—similarly to how it isn't right for a company to skate by on padded financial reports designed to cheat stakeholders and customers. Many of the individuals who led those ventures have died of heart attacks, while others suffer the arguably worse fate of living a large portion of their lives in jail—perhaps with no remorse at all. However, the real casualties in cases like Enron are the employees who lost their jobs and retirement in addition to having the permanent stain of those corporations on their résumés.

It all comes down to ethics. You need people with strong ethics on your team. As a personal message to those who are coming into the corporate world hoping to catch a glimpse of trouble around the curve before it actually reaches your doorstep, I leave you with this: don't feel overburdened by what I'm saying. Yes, there is a spirit of mistrust in the marketplace—I needed to drive that nail home—but the market is a big place. There is still room and time to build a successful company.

I am by no means saying that you are doomed no matter what you do. I'm saying that when you get out there, you must throw everything you've got against the wall and make sure it sticks. Do not be driven by greed. Do the right thing so that you can sleep through the night. Don't be the person whose business is going bankrupt, yet he or she is paying himself or herself an $80 million salary. Heart attacks and jail time is all that comes from that. I've seen it happen, and it's a dangerous road to follow in the name of success and pure greed.

Building a Team

Culture in a company tends to follow what the senior team is doing. The executive management team sets the tone for culture and communication across the board. Nevertheless, I see a lot of companies that are so consumed with their position that they completely forget about the most important thing, which is to have respect for the individual.

Imagine you are standing on a field as a team captain with a set of qualified players before you. Each of these people has gifts, talents, skills, and weaknesses. As a CEO, you are required to lead by example and introduce a vision of change. Like an alchemist, you assess each player. They are a batch of chemicals whose mixture could produce the perfect team or dangerous combustion. You'll have to decide who makes it on the team and who doesn't belong, who will subsidize your weakness and who will augment your strengths. Above all else, you will have to decide who wants to be there, who will give it their all, and who will do it with integrity. After all, this is the place where history is made.

Unfortunately, in this day and age, people are happy to have a job but they aren't always excited about who they work for or the culture that is projected across all angles of the organization. If you aren't hiring people you know—say, a good friend and someone who knows you personally—this is what you will come up against in the job market. Individuals who are good at producing quality work often do it because they are personally and emotionally invested. Those who are doing it because they just want to take home a paycheck are going to play the game of politics, and politics are bad for a company's morale. Employees and stakeholders will smell it a mile away. What you want are people who crave greatness and want to work for a team because of its intrinsic value. Only you can decide who those people are. Surround yourself with successful, knowledgeable people who are driven to achieve success and adapt themselves to a climate of change.

In my opinion, a great team starts with great executives. These individuals must have the power to stir up passion amongst their team members. As leaders, they must enable people to see what they see in the company. If they don't believe in the company, it will be directly reflected in how their team functions. To stand at the helm of my successful business, I want a handful of qualified individuals who have outshone the competition in their fields. I want the best CEO in the industry, the brightest CFO, and on down the line. Overall results and actions need to be at the forefront when making hiring decisions for the benefit of the organization and a great team.

As a global consultant, I walk into a room and face varying structures of executive teams. Some structures work better than others, but this is secondary to how the team works together. I've learned a lot just by observing all of these companies at work. The executive team will make or break your business. What typically breaks a company are CEOs who

- are not involved in the strategy and do not allow the executive team to execute on it;
- don't know their customer base very well;
- are so consumed with holding their position that they forget about having superior customer service;
- hold meetings that meander and drag on;
- lack communication skills;
- don't value their colleagues and team; and
- lack engagement.

What makes a great company are CEOs who

- go see their top customers;
- are involved in day-to-day operations;
- work with their executive team and tackle problems head-on;
- know their company like the back of their hand;
- know what their employees are doing, but do not micromanage;
- have more conversations than presentations;

- are culturally oriented and have a global perspective when considering the needs of their clients and stakeholders; and
- have strong management and advisory teams that enable them to lead and innovate.

In the past six months, I've been asked to represent thirty companies. Out of those, I was forced to turn down twenty-eight because of their business models and practices. I have a standard and a brand to uphold. If CEOs and executive teams are not qualified for the work they are doing, I do not feel comfortable bringing their business to my networks. It would be unfair to everyone involved if I presented unprepared individuals to companies like AT&T, Verizon, Deutsche Telekom, Telecom Italia, and the like. These global organizations would see right through them. The twenty-eight companies I turned down did not convey to me that they were trying to achieve excellence while adding value to their business. Increased revenue streams were the only consideration in those cases.

Why not achieve excellence? Why not make that your mark? No matter what industry you are in, no matter what you build or do, you must be innovative and driven to create a best-in-class organization. Always meet, and strive to exceed, the standards of your industry.

Marketing: The Brick and Mortar of Sales

In my opinion, sales always trumps marketing. Sales is the most important part of a company. It's great to have a Lamborghini as your product, but if it stays on the lot without ever getting sold, then your company fails. Sales is the blood of the company's body, pumping through the veins and carrying out the daily chores. If you don't sell your cruises, your ships will stay in the port; if you don't sell your airline tickets, your planes will never take off. You can have the best marketing in the world, but if there isn't someone there to actually carry out the transaction, you're grounded.

Sales is what drives everything. However, you build a great sales organization by working in tandem with the marketing team. This is the law of sales. Marketing is the brick and mortar for a sales team; sales is the foundation.

Marketing can make you look really good. As a salesman, I take my best step forward when I make friends with the lead marketing representative. Through the years, I have seen marketing groups do what my sales team and I could not do. They organize events and do the wonderful work of bringing people together. They showcase the product and groom the customer for the salesperson to come in and make a sale.

Every year I worked in the telecom world, we had a golf outing, which was completely organized by the marketing group. There were only about a hundred seats, but it was so popular that we always had to turn people away. The marketing team did such an exceedingly great job at putting together the event that all the salespeople had to do was show up and look for their next customer. Imagine what you could do with ten hours on a golf course with your sales targets. Everyone knew we were there to network and eventually make deals, but our customers wanted to come because of the excitement created by the marketing team. I admire marketing teams. When you're fortunate to find a good one, don't let it go.

Integrity

Respect your team members and create success stories while empowering others to grow and succeed. I don't see that in all of the companies I come across, but it must be done. These people spend so much time away from their families that ensuring they are happy in their work environment becomes a critical consideration and undertaking for value and success. It's not a healthy work environment when your employees spend eight to twelve hours a day away from their families and are not enjoying the work that has dragged them away. The majority of us are not running or working for a charity; we are all in this to make money. We all want that hefty commission, but we don't have to get greedy to obtain it.

What else drives you to succeed other than the money and fame? The way I see it, being the CEO of a company with five hundred employees means that I am responsible for five hundred mortgages and the livelihood of all those contributing to the overall success of my business. I believe the key drivers of our economic problems today are greed and a lack of respect for team members, colleagues, and partners. Allow me to illustrate what I mean with an example.

In 2001, while working for Terremark, I was scheduled to have a standard business meeting with the CEO of one of our large telecommunications customers. At the time, he was making $5 million in monthly recurring revenue just from our transport service alone. Our scheduled business meeting went sour after he requested that my company pay him to visit our facility for the meeting. Two years into the sales cycle, I still hadn't convinced him that our business relationship warranted his visit. It didn't matter what I said. He and his team members were extremely negative and turned up their noses at our organization.

Eventually, I was able to schedule a meeting with the company's president of sales. We met in Chicago, and I laid the situation out for her. I let her know that missing our pre-arranged meeting would cost her more than $5 million in monthly recurring charges. She could avoid this altogether by spending the roughly $1,000 monthly recurring cost to collocate in our facility, meet with me, and fulfill the contract requirement—a standard for my company at that time.

Why wouldn't the company take the time to listen to what we were telling them? Were they so self-inflated that they couldn't see the cliff that I was trying to steer them away from? Needless to say, the organization's president of sales promptly signed off on our agreement after meeting with me and hearing my reasoning.

It doesn't matter how big you are, you still have to be humble and listen to people in order to make executive decisions. Exercising stubborn ideas and actions didn't help, because fifteen years later, that company is gone and I'm still here—not behind bars. It turns out that the company's CEO was sentenced to twenty-five years in prison for orchestrating an $11 billion accounting fraud. Was it worth his freedom? You can be the judge of that.

Variables of a Consistent Team

I've shared a bit about CEOs and executive teams. Now, let's talk about the sales team and the 80/20 rule of sales. It is critical that you harness the energy you have and use it to your team's advantage, because if 20 percent of your team is making 80 percent of the sales, then I've got news for you: you're failing.

I once worked with a small business that was fighting an uphill battle managing its sales and resources. The owner came to me with a problem: his sales were not reflecting the time and energy his employees were contributing.

I sat down with him and did some very basic mathematics. Six of his sixteen employees were making 20 percent of the company's sales. They were driven, focused, and had relationships in the industry. They were flying every other week and typically working fourteen-hour shifts. I recommended that the business owner lay off the ten underperforming individuals and compensate the remaining six with more accounts and more money. I urged him to create a support system for those productive few, consisting of more secretaries, more freedom, and more personal gain. The owner bought into my idea and took my recommendations to heart. Each of the six successful salespeople was assigned a small support team. The owner later ended up selling his once small business for millions.

The lesson here is that team members must be consistent. They have to deliver 100 percent of the time or they need to be let go. You can achieve 100 percent success when individuals are working as a team and supporting one another. If one of them isn't successful in an account, he or she can pass it on to the next person who may have a different tactical approach and recover what might have otherwise been lost.

While I strongly support training and retreats, giving your team members defining roles is also important. At retreats, I like to do activities that put two people on a team who otherwise wouldn't get the chance to work so closely together. This way, they have the opportunity to try to understand what the various arms of the company are and what they are responsible for. Bonding occurs that isn't politically motivated and relationships are built that make the office space a more inviting place in which to work.

Definition of functions and full understanding is the key. People get excited when you provide them with training. It inspires them to see the company in a new light and gives them another reason to stay if indeed they were considering a move.

The Athletic Candidate

When it comes to building your team, whether it's marketing or sales, you have to find the right candidates. I work with people I know and their networks. This business floats high on references and referrals, which is why I stress that hard-working people should never burn bridges. Throughout my career, I have found that I work well with athletes. This may be a very personal preference, but I've discovered that athletes are willing to go that extra mile. They are willing to get dirty and do the hard tasks, and do them alongside their teammates. The old saying remains true: "There is no 'I' in team."

I was an athlete—a professional swimmer—for fifteen years. As an athlete, you go through a grueling boot-camp-style schedule. For example, I would swim six days a week, a few hours in the morning and a few in the evening, with school in between. As an athlete, you are forced to become organized, to meet goals every single hour of the day. Soccer players, swimmers, runners—all of them have to beat time, beat their opponents, and strive to further their team.

On your first day in a sales role, you are going to get a quota. It can be $10,000 a month, one hundred iPhones a day, or fifty cruise packages a quarter. We focus our business lives on goals for ourselves and for each other. As a salesperson and an athlete, I know how to set those goals and how to meet them. That is precisely what I am looking for in an employee or, essentially, a teammate.

Creating a Standard of Excellence

It is important for the CEO to create a culture where every contributor on his or her team feels a sense of value and job ownership as well as a level of comfort. It is crucial for a team to feel empowered, recognized, and rewarded as part of the organizational vision and mission at large. Communication is the key to establishing a defined, cohesive culture across all aspects of the organization. Employees must know that they can bring up problems in the workplace with the expectation that these will be handled and resolved. There must also be a clear understanding that every team player has a voice, and constant feedback is valued and accepted. I have seen many teams perform at the corporate level, and not one of them achieved a standard of excellence unless they had built relationships both internally and externally.

When I was young, hardheaded, and in charge, I had a 100 percent success rate when it came to closing deals. I often found myself cleaning up after people who had botched relationships with clients. It was good for the company that I showed such consistency and commitment to continue to build client relationships. So good, in fact, that they gave me my own team to manage. It was my job to oversee their deals and coach them on achieving a stellar success rate. It was also my job to hire and let go many of the people who I wanted on my team.

At the time, I was not as free to admit fault as I am now. We grow and recover faster when we are willing to admit that we've made a mistake. The key is to act proactively instead of reactively. It's a sign of maturity when you can admit fault without thinking that you're coming off as weak. Honesty is always the best policy, and I wasn't able to admit that when it came to teaching my team how to perform. I wasn't good at it at all. There were many times when an account would be handed off to a subordinate, only to have me swoop in at the first sign of trouble, not to coach the team but rather to take on the contract and make the deal myself.

I later learned that the members of my team—the one I was supposed to be leading—were intimidated by my actions and leadership abilities. They were fearful of my management style, and it caused a culture of unrest in the workplace. I was more concerned with gaining a competitive advantage and meeting quotas and sales-revenue objectives than developing a strategic and successful team. Compounding this was added pressure from investors.

I didn't see it this way, however. I ended up firing people and learned some new lessons during the hiring process. I was like a bull in a china shop when it came to asking interview questions. I, of course, knew what I wanted in a team member, but my questions were too direct, too driving. I remember getting kicked under the table many times during interviews by the vice president of human resources (HR), until finally he asked me to undergo some HR coaching and training. I can recall these memories fondly because today we share a mutual professional friendship. We can laugh about these anecdotes and learning experiences.

By the time I was done with HR coaching and training, I welcomed constructive criticism because it made me a better leader. I had to learn tact, and I had to learn how to guide entry-level people without letting my anger get the best of me. It wasn't easy to learn patience on the job, but I did it, and my teams have been better for it ever since.

Admitting your faults is important. It is also imperative to include HR in the day-to-day work that you are doing. When building a team or changing a team structure, no one will help to coalesce a group like HR. Their insight is valuable both on a short- and long-term basis. I understood that their interaction is a great support in order to achieve success. That is why you must depend on everyone, from your executive team to HR, to put forth a united front. This consistent demand for company regulatory standards will encourage individual team members to perform on a competitive level.

Ultimately, I learned that while working as a one-man army and doing all of the deal making myself was good for business, it was bad for the company as a whole. My team wasn't performing, and I wasn't helping them. Most importantly, I needed to learn how to create relationships.

Now you can ask me anything about business and team members, and I'll tell you that the cornerstone to any problem is understanding the relationship. How do you get your executive team and HR to present a united front? If you guessed *relationships*, you are right. Relationships ground individuals in the company and take the focus away from politics. They also promote a vision of change and a cohesive culture that becomes adaptable to the change factor.

Patience

Virtues are important, but there is one that is critical from the moment of an idea's conception to the day you sell your business, and that is patience. Having the wherewithal to invest in a decent stock of patience means everything to the success of your work and mental health. In my more contemplative moments, I have sat down to think about the way conflict arises in my day. In those reflective moments, I am crudely aware of one thing: I am more comfortable being patient with clients, customers, and coworkers than with myself. It is the nature of the business reflected in yourself when driven to achieve success. This realization does not sit well with me. I am extremely patient with my friends who fall short of my expectations and even the waiter who gets my coffee wrong for the hundredth time, yet with myself, I apply a much harsher penalty.

I had to ask myself why was I allowing myself to sit in meetings for hours on end. Why was I spending all of my patience on work while ignoring my own personal needs? In my deep contemplation, I even startled myself. Had I consumed all of my patience so that when I needed it in my own life, there was nothing left to apply?

All I know is that when I fall short of my own expectations, I proceed to beat myself up about it. Slowly, I am coming to the realization that I too deserve patience with myself. I started this book by talking about some of the things I could have done better in the office. I am not perfect, and neither are you. Yet if there is some hardship I can save you in your journey and quest to succeed, it would be this: be patient with yourself and exercise prudence and good judgment. Whatever measure you apply to your work, apply it to yourself. We are only human and life is short.

Be kind to yourself. Be patient with yourself and with others on your team, guiding and leading them on a path to success and fortune. It's well worth the effort. The benefit leads to even greater achievements when handling barriers and human change factors that may affect your overall outcome.

Principle Over Procedure

We've all made early career mistakes on the sales floor—some of us more than others—but I have learned to grow from my mistakes and capitalize on my gains. As a leader, I've had to look policy and procedure in the eye and try to decide when it is best to go by the book and when it is best to go with my gut.

I have always held to a commonsense rule: when making deals, nothing is more important than emotional intelligence. But you can't always teach this stuff. You can't teach people how to think with their gut. Some people have it and some people just don't, which makes it hard to throw out hard-and-fast rules like policy and procedure.

As a leader with this profound intuition, I choose to guide with principle. If you understand the basic nuances of business—meaning you've done your homework and know policies and procedures—then working from a place of common sense where you lean heavily on principle will not be difficult. Some leaders get so lost in procedures that they forget to manage and lead by example. Stick to something that is easy to follow, like an acronym. Give it to your team as a motto and encourage them to remember it. You must be simple and transparent, otherwise your employees will have no direction and will surely get lost. I say lead with COT:

C	**Confidence**	Own your faults with grace and always step up to the plate as a manager without hesitation
O	**Ownership**	Be truthful with your customers and your teams
T	**Transparency**	Have an open-door policy. Be simple and clear in how you run a business and keep the communication channels flowing from top to bottom and vice versa

Reward Your Team

Nothing shows team members that you are interested in retaining them as employees like a great incentive package. Rewards work on everyone—credit cards, children, customers, you name it. Rewards are also a surefire way to ensure that your employees forget about politics and focus on giving your business 100 percent of their efforts.

I once worked with a CEO who believed that his entire team should put health first as one of their goals. It was his thought that healthy bodies made for a healthy company. As such, the company's health care plan was impeccable. He also gave employees full access to a gym. Also, when they went to the doctor, or even took their kids to the doctor, they didn't have to pay anything out of pocket.

Healthy employees were important to this CEO's business, and in turn, maintaining health and their jobs through excellent performance was critical to his employees. The turnover in the company was 0 percent. The employees also had a fantastic 401(k), went on trips when they qualified for President's Circle, and received cash incentives along the way. While some companies will only reward the CEO, this CEO turned it around and gave his team new ways to motivate themselves to succeed.

I look at out-of-the-box thinkers like that CEO and know that if you are starting a business, or starting new in an old business, you have to do it on the right foot. Make sure your employees are happy. As a leader, it is always possible to do this. You simply have to listen and be willing to commit to creating relationships.

I once witnessed the exact opposite at an organization. I worked with a company who hired a new CEO following a merger of two large companies where the bigger of the two swooped in and started to change things. The first thing that occurred was the very thing that eventually drove the employees out the door. The CEO saw that the employees were comfortable and enjoyed great health care, incentives, and trips. He decided this was a soft corporate culture. To firm it up, he reduced the benefit package drastically. He even cut salaries. The organization went into an uproar, and almost immediately, people started to leave. To remedy the situation, the CEO tried hiring new people to replace those who left, but the culture was never the same. The company suffered very high turnover because the employees no longer felt valued and part of a cohesive culture.

As you assemble and lead your team, establishing trust, maintaining integrity, leading by principle, and rewarding and incentivizing your employees should be topline elements of your managerial style. It is the difference between success and failure as an organization.

CHAPTER 7

Business Is Personal

Making business personal means getting creative in your approach to business development. How do you seek out the next deal? How do you respond in the moment with a wise decision? Creativity is the glue that holds together the technical elements of your work. Don't be afraid to get personal, creative, and improvisational in your business development and deal-making activities.

I recall once trying to secure a meeting with a company whose name I won't use. Getting a meeting with this particular CEO was next to impossible. For whatever reason, this guy did not want to make time to sit down and hear my ideas.

This isn't an uncommon barrier in business. We all spend lots of time trying to get the attention of the person who will help make our next big break. For me, it was this CEO. I knew I had to get creative in order to secure my meeting with him. My goal was simply to explain how a partnership between our two companies would benefit us both.

First, I did my research. I found out from a source that this particular CEO was going to be flying from Miami to Los Angeles on a specific day and time—a six- to eight-hour flight. My task at that point was to find out what airline he was flying and what seat he would be sitting in. If you're thinking these are extreme measures, you don't know how important it is to be aggressive and determined to close a deal. I'm the guy who has signed contracts on the hoods of cars and elevator doors.

I was willing to bet that going over the top in this particular situation would get me the result that I needed.

When the time came, I was already on the flight and seated by the time the CEO boarded the plane. When he saw me, his jaw dropped, and his eyes lit up. I had eight hours to convince him of my strategy, but it took only fifteen minutes. Going in, I knew two things: what I wanted from him and what I had to produce to convince him I was right. I had already set the goal, and all that was left was follow-through.

Fifteen minutes after the plane took off, I'd already met my goal. For the rest of the flight, we chatted about his kids, sports, and inflight entertainment. In the airport afterward, I continued to follow his moves and watched him make his first phone call to his executive team to relay the news. Subsequently, I discovered that I would be working with the executive team in the months to come, and not the CEO directly. But because the order came from him, I knew that his team would be open and willing to work with me.

Straight Shooters

A straight shooter is someone who knows how to be direct and aggressive without being rude. I climbed aboard that plane because I knew the importance of one-on-one meetings. You may think that being trapped in a seat while I proceeded with my sales pitch would have made the CEO angry or made him withdraw from our conversation. It might have, if I wasn't smart about it. But I've learned that being aggressive doesn't always mean being intimidating. I never want clients to feel intimidated, but if they know what lengths I went through to speak to them, then that element of pursuit should express my seriousness about the business relationship. It is all in the approach.

Yes, I had the upper hand in that situation, and I could have scared him off with my element of surprise, but I didn't. I was there to be personable. I was there to be warm and show the human side of my business. This personal touch has always been and will always be invaluable.

A straight shooter doesn't beat around the bush, but rather identifies a target and pursues it until completion. It's a systematic approach.

The reason I am so dedicated to it is because I value my time. I don't like businesspeople who keep going around and around in circles. It's nauseating and endless. Remember the real estate agent I mentioned earlier? The first one who didn't have real answers for me? She was a waste of my time.

I've had many people seek me out for meetings. What I want and what I respect is the person who finally gets me alone and is straightforward, not passive. Tell me what you are going to deliver and then follow through with it. Within ten minutes of our conversation, I should know what you want, what you need to accomplish, and what role I am playing in your strategy. The best way for this to happen is to discuss it during a one-on-one meeting.

When outlining the elements of an effective approach to being a successful straight shooter, I think we all can come up with a short list that suits our work style. Some would say the best thing is to be approachable, articulate, and authentic—the three As. Others swear by the three Cs—calm, cool, and collected. I have a friend who lives by the mantra of being both communicative and disciplined. Your personal mantra and approach should be a direct reflection of your personality.

Whatever your personal style, always remember to be personable, approachable, and articulate. If you can couple those things with those that appear on my short list below, you've got a great combination that will get you results. Straight shooters demonstrate the following:

- stamina
- aggressiveness
- decisive decision making
- team building
- deliberate objectives in meetings

The willingness to be aggressive and not take no for an answer have aided me when I've had to soothe client accounts that were mishandled by other employees who did not have a clue about what they were doing.

Goal Setting

How do I make deals? I've stated before that relationships are what set the social stage for that to happen. Learning to be personable, relaxing into the role—all of that goes into being a people person and building relationships. The other side to closing deals is setting a goal of what you want to accomplish.

If I wanted to sell an idea to a corporate giant like AT&T but did not have a clue of how to do it, I would work backward from the goal. Working backward from the goal entails the following:

- Be specific.
- Make sure your pitch/value is measurable.
- Identify the source.
- Do your research and introduce checks and balances.
- Outline your approach.
- Follow through and exercise accountability.
- Find common ground.

To summarize, make business personal, get creative, and be a straight shooter with stamina who sets goals. Not many deals are made overnight. But if you're communicative, disciplined, and willing to go the extra mile, you'll consistently hit the targets on which you set your sights.

CHAPTER 8

The Importance of Relationships

As a businessman, I wish I could say that money is the fuel that keeps this world spinning on its axis. But after flying millions of miles from point A to point B and back again, and witnessing and being a part of business transactions, I can honestly say that nothing moves a pen across the signature section of a contract like the power of connection and continued relationships.

Previously, I mentioned the deep connectedness and emotional stake I felt when I discussed products. It used to be that business was as simple as forking over cash for an item you wanted or needed; the transaction was easy and emotionless. But now, there are so many products floating around out there that in order to stay relevant, companies must become likeable to customers. Companies seeking the likeability factor go so far as to plaster "Go Green" or "Organic" or "Gluten-Free" stickers on their products. Driven to start a conversation, they tap into the emotional reservoir of their customers.

Historically, being a business partner was as easy as dropping off a shipment, collecting your check, and driving away with pockets full of cash. But today, the market has changed and grown. Now there is a global market with multiple avenues for the right businesses to sell goods while competing on a much broader level. If a business wants to remain relevant in its customers' eyes, it has to employ people who are likable, who can maintain a conversation and work to build trust within their common networks.

Understanding different cultures and business demands is also key to becoming a global sales consultant. I'll admit that when I look at a résumé, I am not just looking at experience and schooling; I am also concerning myself with the candidate's network and achievements. Who does the candidate know, and what industry has the individual covered? Does the candidate have experience integrating business exposure on both a national and an international level?

Let this be a lesson that critical business relationships matter. They are now the vitality to your business, because relationships matter more now than they ever did. They drive the success of your business. What people think of you today will impact the work they are willing to pursue with you tomorrow. With increasing prosperity, it is through our networks that we make the best deals and generate successful revenue streams.

On the one hand, customers want to feel something when they purchase an item; on the other, businesspeople want to know they are working with others who are likeable and have common business sense. Silly is the businessperson who thinks that he or she can walk into a meeting and command attention simply by looking the part and overloading executives with nonsense. If you are unable to open your mouth and befriend people, your facade of glamour will fall flat. Keep in mind that business relationships are the new currency when dealing on a global platform. Build trust and create a sense of ownership.

Business Relationships Start with Icebreakers

Icebreakers are critical to establishing a connection and fostering trust with business prospects, never more so than when cold calling or repairing a damaged customer relationship or troubled account.

I remember a time when I was placed on an account that someone else had already started to bungle. I showed up to the executive's office and was asked to wait. I sat down, and slowly, one minute turned into fifteen. I was convinced that the client was in no rush to speak with me. He may have even been ready to let the account go and work with someone else.

Two things were against me in this situation. The first was that I was beginning this relationship from a negative perspective and track record. The second was that these were the circumstances under which I was meeting this executive for the very first time and doing damage control. Cold contact—and I had to get him to like me so that I could convince him of my plan to save the account and continue to do business together.

Rethinking my plan, I looked around his waiting room to see if we had any common interests to bring up in conversation. I didn't see anything. His walls were all but blank, and the few pictures were very abstract modern things I knew nothing about.

On a tray in the corner of his office there was a cistern of water. I got up, walked over, and poured myself a glass. Next to the cups, there was a Rubik's Cube. I like puzzles, so I scooped it up and quickly sifted through the tiles one by one until each side was a uniform color: white, red, green, orange, blue, and yellow.

The door opened, and the man stormed in. I stood up confidently, still unsure of how I would be received. As I followed him into his conference room, I noticed him eyeing the toy that was still in my hand.

"Oh, it's nothing," I said. "I just found this in your office."

He sat behind his desk, gesturing for me to sit down as well. "Let me see it," he said with his palm up and hovering.

Before sitting, I leaned forward and placed it in his hand. "I like puzzles, so I just thought I would attempt to pull that off before our meeting."

"You didn't do this, did you?" He looked at me with an expression of disbelief.

"I did," I reassured him.

"Then you can do it again." He rapidly took the Rubik's Cube and spun it out of proportion. The tiles were back to their original state. He held the block up to eye level. "Now do it."

I love this kind of thing. I grinned quickly and chuckled a little bit, shrugged, and reached for the cube. "Okay, I'll give it a try."

As I spun the chunks of plastic in a frenzy, I began to talk to him about why I was there. I needed him to hear me out and help me with my plan to fix the account and lead our business venture to a successful outcome. Within minutes, he stopped me from talking. His eyes were transfixed on the Rubik's Cube in my hands. I could see amazement on his face.

"You did it again!" he said with excitement. "I've never seen anyone do that before, and so fast!"

And with that, I knew I had found my icebreaker.

He never forgot the Rubik's Cube trick, and we were able to work together to save the account because I'd earned his trust. He had a reason to like me. Key consideration needs to be given to the fact that finding a common understanding and interest is valuable when meeting a business prospect and delivering your sales pitch.

Whether the common interest is a specific magazine on your prospect's desk, a photograph or painting on his or her office walls, or a Rubik's Cube, establish a connection by breaking the ice through any means readily at hand.

Building Working Relationships

Recently, I received news that a global executive and customer of mine passed away. The news of his passing sparked a flood of great emotion within me. I'll call him Frank for now, and I can say that in our fifteen years of knowing each other, we often worked together on large deals for his companies in a global setting. We would arrange meetings with the intent of discussing business and signing contracts, but the business portion of our talks would only last ten to fifteen minutes.

After we got that out of the way, we would lapse into a zone of comfort and ease. I would ask him about his kids. Over the years, I would hear of them getting into soccer camps, finally applying for colleges, and getting scholarships. We would talk about family and really get to know each other in the little time we had to work together.

I met Frank because I was trying to win business from Telecom Italia. I went into his office unarmed and without strategy; my only intent was to make his acquaintance. We bonded over the fact that I could speak Italian. That served as the icebreaker to our long-lasting relationship. Through the bond of language, we began to form a connection.

Eventually, he introduced me to people in my field who would help shape me and create the Telecom Italia deal I desired. That agreement and deal brought $10 million of revenue to Terremark Worldwide.

Looking back at our first interactions now, I know with all of my heart that Frank would not have worked with me had he not felt some kind of connection with me. In building relationships, it is often that first icebreaker that will open or close doors.

Frank believed that he could put his network into my hands and that I would take care of those relationships that he cared so much about. He became my mentor and good friend. We discussed trade shows and my career goals, and we would go to the same restaurant every time he visited New York. Eventually, I had the chance to turn that around and help him when he needed me because of some unforeseen circumstances. When I started BVS Consulting, Frank was the first to sign on as a future board member. Regrettably his advisory expertise and valued contribution lasted only a few months.

After running into customers at trade shows, after meetings with them and placing calls to their personal phones, you run out of business things to talk about. You cross a line that allows you to reveal bits and pieces of your lives. At some point, your relationship becomes personal, and it would behoove you to go along with that and reap the benefits.

Frank knew I was writing a book, and he knew I was starting a company. He supported me no matter what. He personally had great confidence in my dedication to our work together. While his passing has affected me in a very emotional way, my coworkers tended to only focus on the business side of things. Frank had obligations to our business and built a powerful relationship. As our champion in various business ventures, he made promises to help set things up and continue to increase our revenues.

Now that he is gone, we must decide how to move forward with his account and drive the business forward. On one side, I am saddened by the loss of my dear friend, but on the other, Frank was originally a work acquaintance who shared many things in common with me. It was through our working relationship that we became friends, which led to him becoming an even greater mentor to me over these many years.

CHAPTER 9

Relational Intelligence

Relational intelligence is the harnessing of basic people skills to lead others into relating to you on a personal level. It is being authentic and open with people. What enables me to build long-term relationships like the one I fostered with my friend Frank—and also short, passing relationships like the one I built with Mr. Rubik's Cube—is my ability to harness my relational intelligence. When you are practicing relational intelligence, you are actively negotiating social spaces in an effort to create profitable bonds with others. To be prosperous in your new relationships, focus on the following:

- establishing trust and ownership
- delivering consistent results—leading with the willingness to give instead of simply receive
- offering support
- showing authenticity and even vulnerability
- keeping in touch and constantly following up
- informing customers of your successes through newsletters, published articles, press releases, and social media
- developing ongoing collaborations and coalitions

The truth is that we are all connected to each other in some way or another. I believe the rule is something like six degrees of separation between each of us. So the work of fostering relationships with people is not in being connected to someone else in particular, it's what you choose to do with that connection.

Legal Considerations

The Latin proverb *Verba volant, scripta manent*, or "Spoken words fly away, written words remain," became my dictum when I started in sales. My knowledge of Latin helped me in two profound ways: it enabled me to learn more languages, and it gave me this quotable reminder that all of my work would amount to smoke if I didn't get it down on paper to sign, seal, and deliver a deal. Language skills helped in breaking barriers and building connections with others. You may think I'm talking about this book, which is applicable, but I'm also referring to the legal world of contracts.

Contracts serve the purpose of outlining the relationship between two companies. There is no way either company can get to work without the contract. Think of it as the rulebook of a football game. A contract sets boundaries for a working relationship and establishes a fair way of overcoming mishaps whenever a disagreement occurs. It also includes provision rights, obligations, and services provided—a document of expectations for both parties.

The goal of every salesperson is to get to the contract stage of the discussion. Once you have a soft yes, you get the lawyers involved to iron out the particulars of the deal. As someone whose quota depends on the signing of the contract, it is my top priority to make sure that both parties, their company and mine, reach an amicable agreement and build consensus. You can spend all the time you want talking about a deal, but unless you close and put it to paper, you will not receive compensation for your time, craft, and patience.

With lawyers involved, what is a global salesperson's role in the contract phase? When it comes to contracts, there are many places where your hard work can come to a full stop. It all comes down to communication. Throughout my experience, I learned that I had to be the one greasing the wheels to keep the machine of lawyers, executives, and other voices working together. I always set myself up as the go-between contact for the lawyers and the client. After all, I was the one who built relationships with each of the team members. Eventually, I made myself known to my clients' lawyers and always made it a point to befriend the individual.

I am the first to agree that lawyers can be a tough crowd. I know this because for two years, I attended law school. However, that is what they're paid to do—be aggressive for the sake of their client. My role as the executive is twofold: liaison and translator. As a good liaison, I enhance the way the two parties communicate and interact. When it comes to the actual contract, I serve as a translator, interpreting and rewording legal jargon in order to clarify and incorporate business terminology to smooth out the entire process. Every business deal needs a contract, but I've seen months of work get stalled because the contract can't be signed and introduces many barriers.

Take, for instance, a contract I received from a client in Brazil. My lawyer sent me the contract, and I in turn sent it to the client. The customer spent a few days on it and sent it back to me. When I took a look at it, I cringed. The piece they sent back looked like a lit-up Christmas tree. As I looked at the amalgamation of items underlined in various colors and flagged words, I felt my heart—and my hope for a quick close—sinking slowly. If I sent that back to my lawyer as it was, I could expect to get it back in about six months, no kidding. That's six months too long to wait to iron out the details of how our two parties would be working together. So I set myself to untangling the Christmas-tree lights.

The philosophy I have is to keep my clients' lawyers happy just like I have to keep my lawyer happy. If by chance their lawyer doesn't like me, I can promise you that I'm not moving forward and getting anywhere in the agreement quickly. I start making moves to get to know their lawyer as early as the first meeting with their executive team. When our groups get together, I casually suggest we invite the lawyer to come to lunch with us. "Is Frederick available?"

It has happened often enough that a "Frederick" will dine with our teams and I'll learn something interesting about him. For example, if Frederick is a soccer fan, I'll say, "Frederick, I actually have tickets to that game, you should come with me. I don't know anyone here." Who wouldn't want to see Messi, the best soccer player in the world, playing live in Barcelona?

We'll spend another afternoon in each other's company, becoming friendly. Within three days, I can promise you that "Frederick" will have put together a contract and will have it sitting on my desk or airplane tray table. "Frederick" represents a contract that is a multimillion-dollar deal, and through simple human engagement, I've decimated any walls of defensiveness that may have kept our two companies from working together in a relatively short time. Dear reader, relationships are everything.

There are many different situations on which a contract can get snagged—things as small as the format of the contract or as large as when the initial payment is due. Everything has to be addressed in the contract stage, and I couldn't do it without my three As and three Cs.

As an example, when a contract comes back to me looking like a Christmas tree, I phone their lawyer and say, "We need to take a look at sections 1E, 3C, and 4F." Sometimes this leads to a conference call with both parties on the line—but you see what I'm doing. I'm taking the initiative and pioneering the changes in the contract so that when my lawyer has it for final review, he has a document that isn't cluttered with jargon. It is a clear and concise agreement, one that I know he can sign off on. This makes a process concrete without any consideration for both short- and long-term obstacles that might derail a great deal.

CHAPTER 10

Book Smarts vs. Street Smarts

We tend to think of book smarts and street smarts as opposite sides of a spectrum—if you have one, you do not have the other. However, what ultimately pulls these two opposites together is emotional intelligence. Emotional intelligence is the glue; it is the stuff that I've been preaching about since page 1 of this book. Emotional intelligence will help you take those facts that you learned in school and use them to your advantage. Relying on a mix of book smarts and street smarts will allow you to foster important relationships, build your network, and tackle those sweet, sweet deals you've been dreaming of.

Résumés

Nowadays, I'm the guy who reviews the résumés—but it wasn't always like that. I used to be in your shoes, wondering how much of my experience really mattered when compared to the degree I earned. It's a good question, and one that has plagued mankind since the dawn of business. Academics are nice, but how much do they help you in the real world? To me, this is the difference between book smarts and street smarts.

Students often ask me about their résumés. They want to know how to format them and dress them up so that their accomplishments pop off the page. They ask me whether internships and volunteerism will actually help them to secure the job and the paycheck that they want. I tell them the following story.

When I was about eighteen, my heart swelled with the desire to give back to the community. I wanted to change the world. I've always had a talent for languages, so I signed up with Amnesty International and soon became a translator for the Human Rights Committee. In the three years I worked for Amnesty International, I flew around Eastern Europe until the very end of my journey.

I think any one of us may look back on our youth and wonder if we wasted our time giving away free hours when we could have been building our sandcastles and empires. When I was building my résumé after the tour, I looked back on my years with Amnesty and decided that these were in fact important years that showcased my ability to speak languages and become an effective leader. Even if it didn't help me in the long run, I had still been true to myself and followed a path I felt I needed to be on. I added Amnesty International to my résumé and never looked back.

Fast-forward to my early thirties, when I was working with Jamie. Remember, this is a woman who never once looked at my résumé. I walked through her door and she could smell the street smarts on me. My résumé could have been a tabloid for all she cared; she never gave it much thought. I was trying to win a very big project with a chairman of a big corporation in New York. He was impressed with what Jamie had to say about me. Other references sent him glowing remarks, which was good for me, but wasn't quite securing the deal. He still wanted to meet with me. He still wanted to go over my résumé to see if I was the right man for the job.

We sat down at a restaurant for a meal while he reviewed my résumé. I can still hear him asking, "Oh, you worked for Amnesty International?" It brought an upswing to his voice and introduced a turn in our otherwise flat conversation.

By this time, it had been at least ten years since my volunteer duties with Amnesty. "Yes, but a long, long time ago," I answered slowly, wondering where this could be going.

"That's interesting. I'm on the board."

Of course, I was surprised. Here he was picking up on a minute detail of my résumé that was leading us into an engaging conversation.

Emotional intelligence is the stuff that will allow a listener to follow someone down an unknown rabbit hole. His next question was with whom I remembered working. I named a few people, but ultimately came upon the name of Scott Long, a Harvard graduate with a specialty in human rights.

"Oh, you know Scott Long?" There was clear excitement in his voice. I could tell that he respected Scott a lot. I couldn't blame him; I thought well of him too. "So, if I call Scott up right now, will he remember you?"

That was the button to push. I guess it was really up to chance then. If Scott did remember me, I could only hope he had more than simple things to say about me. The chairman was really putting me on the spot, but I decided to push forward. "Why don't you give Scott a call? Let's find out what he says about me," I replied.

Sure enough, he got Scott on his cell. I could only see the CEO and Amnesty board member's face. He wasn't very expressive but he nodded along. I sat in my chair, a bit squeamish, wondering if I should be worried. It was an odd turn in our conversation. I have to say that in all of my years of keeping Amnesty on my résumé, this had never happened before.

I had no idea if Scott would remember me or have positive things to say about me, but he did. He was actually excited to hear that I was sitting in front of this chairman and CEO and that I was in a position to make these kinds of deals. The chairman hung up the phone, and the interview was over at that point. We sat, ate, and let the conversation move on to other things. The man hired me, and our relationship only grew from that time onward.

In the end, it was important for me to have that experience with Amnesty because even though it didn't reflect on my current professional abilities, it set me up with a network I never knew I would need again. Street smarts will show that in order to establish a relationship, you often have to follow the lead of the other person.

Be friendly, trust your gut, and put those electives on your résumé. Show that you know people who aren't just in your business field. It will go a long way.

Interviews

This business isn't for everyone. There is a science to getting someone to like you. Some people are just naturally likeable, while others are not. If you're not one of those people who is easily liked, who can work their way around the room and come out the other side having shaken hands and made friends, there is still hope for you. I won't say the business world isn't for you. I still believe that you can fake it until you make it. Just remember my three As and three Cs.

In my story above, I could have become outwardly nervous when the chairman and CEO decided to ask me about a portion of my résumé I hadn't talked about in years. I could have showed him how flustered it made me and even asked him not to call Scott Long. After all, I knew that the other people who had given me recommendations were going to say glowing things about me. I had no idea what Scott would say; he was a wild card. But you know what? I stayed calm. I kept my cool. I was collected as the chairman and CEO made the call. Keeping my composure served to reinforce the things he'd already noticed about me: that I was articulate and knowledgeable about the deal I was proposing and that I was approachable and authentic too. I wasn't giving up on making my deal, and I was going to make sure that the chairman and CEO knew that.

I talk a lot about being aggressive. I think it's one of my favorite words in business. To be relentless means that there is no obstacle or climate that can keep you from focusing on your goal. You will see the goal through a haze and through an obstruction in your path. I do feel that at this point, however, I need to make sure that when I say "aggressive," you're not thinking *pigheaded* and *rude*. I'll tell you about a job applicant who mixed up those concepts, but first, let me digress for a moment to introduce a belief of mine that will be important to the story.

As a leader in my field, I must admit that I wouldn't be able to get much done in my day without my assistant. She often knows more about what is going on in the company than I do. By this, I mean that she is juggling my schedule and speaking to my legal team as well as the many consultants who filter in and out of my office. She manages so many things for me that often, I just sign off on daily tasks because I trust her so implicitly.

If she comes to me and says, "Ben, you should talk to this person," then I will stop what I am doing and get on the phone. On the other hand, if she approaches me and says, "I just need to let you know that this other person has been calling you," I know there is no urgency, that she is informing me just to keep me abreast of the situation. We have developed a language, and she knows what needs to get done at the end of the day. Many things don't even come to my attention.

In order for her to do her job, she has to know about the relationships I'm building and the work I am doing. She has to be my partner in crime, and oftentimes, my second brain. Nothing gets to me unless it goes through her first, and because I know that about my relationship with her, I know that other C-level executives are doing the same thing.

For this reason, when I reach out to important C-level executives, it is crucial that I get acquainted with their assistants. I know you may think this is a strategy you only see in the movies, but one of the true ways to an executive is through his or her assistant. Sometimes you won't even get the chance to speak to the executive. You will be working through his or her assistant.

Experience tells me that assistants are a crucial factor in running successful companies. Befriending them will help get you in touch with their legal teams as well as any other department you need to touch base with in order to get your job done. Nobody wants to admit that the assistants are often the ones running the companies, but if you keep this bit of information in the back of your mind, you will know how to get what you want when you are managing an account.

However, it's not just assistants that will help you hunt the "big dog"—that major executive. Think broadly about what I am telling you. Think about the people who are close in business to the person you are trying to work with. They can be the concierge at the hotel who has the ear of the manager or even the staff person who knows how the airline really does booking. What I am hoping you will see is that you don't always have to go for the top-tier person. Trying to get that individual's attention can be exhausting. Find out where that executive gets his or her information from, and that's the person you want on your team. It works every single time.

Being introduced by a person of trust establishes credibility in ways that a cold-contact greeting cannot. That's how you get into a room, but when you are given an opportunity to meet with the executive, practice skills of emotional intelligence, not emotional blackmail. Here is an example of the difference between the two.

I was once interviewing a gentleman from Qwest Communications. I really liked him because he was articulate and smart. He also came with great connections and recommendations, so I believed he could be part of my team. However, toward the end of the interview, he started to get a little aggressive. We all know I like this word and respond well to anyone who shows energy, so I heard him out.

"Listen," he prodded, "you should really hire me." He then proceeded to lay out the three other offers that companies had made him. "If you don't hire me today, I'll have to move on to these three other offers, you understand."

I understood, but I also wasn't ready to make a move and hire someone—even someone I liked—without first talking to my team. I needed to talk to my CEO and HR at the least. So I told him we would have to wait, and I would get back to him about the job.

As we wrapped up the meeting, I found myself retracting from our conversation. Whatever rapport he had established with me quickly diminished as he fought for a job offer right there on the spot. I ushered him out of my office, trying to trace back to the moment that really turned me off. It was the way he became emotionally manipulative once he discovered that I liked him.

No executive likes to be pushed around, and that's exactly how I felt. The meeting had ended coldly because of his pushiness. It's interesting, though, because he was aware enough to read the situation and know that I was responding favorably to his résumé. Whatever signals I was sending him relayed the truth that I was an employer who was impressed with what he could bring to my team. I had even begun to imagine the impact he could have in our department. Yet he didn't give me the chance to make him an offer. He jumped the gun, and when I finally got him out of my office, I decided I wouldn't be calling him back. Although he had the skills that I needed, I'd lost faith in him the moment he gave me an ultimatum.

The truth is he was following the road map I lay for myself when encountering new deals:

1. Establish a relationship.
2. Use emotional intelligence.

I didn't like that he used what he knew about the meeting to try to pin me in a corner. As I thought about it, I realized his approach to step 2 was really to use emotional blackmail, not emotional intelligence. I moved on, and he lost a great job opportunity.

Fast-forward a few days. I was in London for meetings. Travel days are usually very important days for me because I am using all of my time and energy to get to know both the executive I will be working with and his or her team. My assistant, who doesn't accompany me on these trips, doesn't bring trivial things to my attention on travel days unless they are very important.

I was leaving a meeting in London accompanied by my CEO Jamie when I received one of those calls from my assistant. Even through the phone, I could hear that she was particularly upset. This was so unlike her that I turned to the group and asked if they had a private room I could step into. Once alone, I hunched over the phone, wondering what could possibly have gotten my champion of an assistant to call me in such an unraveled state.

"Ben, I have this gentleman on the line, and he's threatening me."

My mind drew a blank. Who on earth would have the wherewithal to threaten my assistant? "Who are you talking about?" I asked.

"The guy from the interview a few days ago," she said, jogging my memory. "He's been calling, and now he really wants to speak to you. He's threatening this and that, he won't wait until you are back on Friday, and he's demanding to speak to Jamie." Her voice jolted, and I could tell she was about to break.

The hairs on my neck were standing on end. Who was this guy, and why did he think he could harass anyone he was seeking a job with? I was angry, but I soon realized that we could deal with the situation very easily. My first move was to soothe my assistant.

"Listen," I said, and I waited until her breathing had calmed because I wanted her to grasp the full weight of my words. "Don't let anyone make you feel like you are beneath them. You still run an organization for me."

I could hear her breaths coming in a slower, more natural rhythm and imagined the tears receding from her eyes. I meant it. She really was an asset to the entire company, not just me. I wanted to discipline the guy for making her feel like that. The thought ran through my head to hire him only to send him on some impossible goose chase and then fire him. Yet there were so many factors involved. I didn't want to do anything that could get us sued, so I told her to get HR to send him a rejection letter immediately. I didn't care if it was hand-delivered the same day. I just wanted to have in writing that we were not interested in hiring him, and to do that in a way that was calm and professional.

Furthermore, I told my assistant that as soon as she received delivery confirmation for that letter, she had my permission to call him up and put him in his place. I wanted her to say whatever she needed to, within reason. She went back to him and let him know that he'd failed his interview and that he'd messed it up long before she ever got involved; by harassing her, he was in fact harassing her boss who was, in her words, the "golden boy" of the company.

This guy did all that he could to burn bridges. He could have won us over with his approach or with his personality, with his personal As and Cs, but he bungled it every step of the way. His ego was so big that he couldn't be mindful of what was going on in the room around him.

When students ask me about the contributing factors in making deals, I always think about emotional intelligence, but what I really mean when I say that is you have to have balance. You have to look at your arsenal of weapons—including everything you learned as a kid in school and the experience you picked up in volunteer hours—and be savvy about which of those cards you play when you are encountering new people and new situations. Be honest, authentic, and articulate, because emotional intelligence means harnessing the discerning qualities that give you empathy when analyzing situations and relationships.

Some would call this just having a sense of social awareness. That man had the skill, the network, and the experience, but he didn't have the brains to maintain relationships.

When you were a kid, you may have been taught how to be polite when around company and to close the door gently after you exited a room. I can hear mothers across America saying, "Shut the door—don't slam it." You may have been taught how to be a good loser: "Don't pout and throw a tantrum," "Leave the field and shake your opponent's hand," or "Good game, good game." It's hard to believe that those lessons we learned as kids are often mistaken as lessons that only belong in our youth. I'm here to say that those rules we learned as eight- and nine-year-olds are still applicable in our lives today, especially in the business world.

The offices of professionals can seem more like a sports field than an office space. We are so competitive that we often forget that the people we are dealing with today could very well be our teammates tomorrow. We forget to be polite and to leave a position with grace, having maintained relationships instead of burning bridges.

Not many years ago, the telecom world suffered a huge hit. The economy was in a recession, and there were few businesses that were doing very well. I watched the market get cut down in size. Telecom businesses were falling by the wayside one by one, and those that weren't going under were laying off employees in droves.

I sat on a few accounts with my CEO, Jamie. We were accustomed to swooping into places that needed our products and working closely with teams of customers, but their offices started to feel empty after a while. People were being let go, and we found ourselves working with smaller and smaller teams. Only the best employees were hanging on. We had to make sure that there was a spirit of camaraderie in the teams we assembled. Our goal, every time we got to a new sales floor, was to build relationships and make sure the competition that once existed between these groups was kept at bay.

Don't get me wrong, these were all salespeople who at one time or another had been my competitors as well, but Jamie and I found ourselves leading groups successfully because we had a secret.

Prior to the economic crash, Jamie and I had a system. Whenever we signed a deal with a new company, we made sure to work with more than just the executive to whom we'd originally been introduced. Yes, the executive was our champion and we needed that person to be in our corner, but we were also aware of the fact that it takes an entire team to move the ball forward. What would happen to our account if our champion was fired or moved to a competitor? If the champion lost his or her position, we would have no connection to the company. The progress we made on the account would have to be restarted, and that's not an easy job.

Going forward with contracts, both Jamie and I decided to build relationships with the entire team. This was very casual. It meant that when we traveled, we didn't get out of the meetings and hibernate in our hotel rooms. Rather than having personal time, we spent those hours with the team. We invited them out for a drink or dinner. We spent hours getting to know them or just blowing off steam at the end of the day. Building those relationships allowed us to make friends in places we later relied on when the crash occurred. While everyone else in the industry had built walls around their teams, we'd made enough friends to keep our business alive as the economy sank to its knees.

This is a simple illustration of the balance that must be kept. Balancing relationships is just as important as making the deal. Where would Jamie and I have been if we didn't treat people with respect, and even befriend competitors we were working with? We would have lost deals and missed the opportunity to create the kinds of sales teams that eventually saved our business. To me, balance means being mindful of your strengths, your weaknesses, and the things you can't control. You can't control the economy, or whether the person with whom you established your contract will get fired or quit. What you can do is invest in people. After all, it is relationships that will last, even after a business has gone bankrupt.

So, at the end of your workday, remember to cultivate those work relationships, even if it means stretching across the aisle. Yes, there is power in competition, but there is longevity in collaboration.

Getting Your Foot in the Door

Some would say I am an expert in recruitment—I screen anywhere between 2,000 to 3,000 résumés a year. When an executive is reviewing résumés at that rate, you may be interested to know what his or her process is in choosing one résumé over another. After all, a résumé is the only thing you have to differentiate yourself from the hundreds of other people applying for that same job. So, how does an executive go about picking ten people to interview out of a stack of a thousand résumés? It's a time-consuming job. Ultimately, what an executive wants to end up with is a pile of résumés that exhibit a conglomeration of academic achievement and demonstrated work ability.

How does one get there? Well, the first thing any executive like myself will do is pull the résumés from Harvard, Columbia, and Wharton, to name a few. Every now and again, I will look at candidates without an Ivy League education and place their résumé in the "interview" pile because of the experience shown, but it's a smaller percentage. Candidates with master's degrees from prestigious business schools will make up the majority of my reading material. I will look long and hard at about a hundred of these résumés, and from there, I will invite about ten of those candidates into my office. While eight of those candidates will have acquired an Ivy League MBA, the two remaining candidates will have some level of education, a great network, and the kind of experience that far outweighs the fact that they didn't go to an Ivy League school.

Why don't all of the people who went to an Ivy League school get the job? Just because you have book smarts doesn't mean you have common business sense, and common sense is a large part of street smarts. We all admire the work of Ivy League graduates because they are highly intelligent people, but I can't look beyond the fact that sometimes that system fails. Let me reinforce the fact that I support academia in a very big way, considering my involvement in this sector when lecturing across the globe.

From that group of eight individuals, a few of the candidates will enter my office and I will know within five seconds that I am not interested in hiring them. I remember speaking with a qualified candidate from

Harvard who studied international law. We were looking for someone who would be able to fly to London and other European cities once or twice a week. This candidate sitting in my office passed the interview with flying colors, only to end the discussion on a sour note. "Will I need a passport to go to London?" she asked. A big mistake!

I couldn't believe this was someone who'd received a degree from Harvard. There she was, an intelligent candidate who had gotten into a prestigious school and graduated with all the bells and whistles an MBA could afford, yet she did not have the common sense to explore the facts of traveling abroad. This candidate was one of ten people in a thousand to get a foot in my door, and she ruined her only opportunity.

My question to qualified candidates is, what makes anyone think that just because they made it to a good school, they can ignore the world around them? Thinking globally is the key consideration in this case. To those who are in Ivy League schools now, and to those young entrepreneurs who will never have the opportunity to do so, my message is the same. You are your own best asset, and therefore you must think outside the box and on a global scale.

Getting to Where You Want to Be

I say this to you because it is what I believe myself: I am my own best asset. Yes, I can speak six languages. Seven, actually, because I am in the process of learning Portuguese. Yes, I also went to a good school. I say yes to all of the things that make me look like a good candidate on paper –but those aren't the only things that make me my own best asset.

What makes me my own best asset is the fact that I will accomplish, I will achieve, and I will do and commit, because I believe in myself. If you took all of my achievements away from me today—my networks, résumé, business, and money—and dropped me in China in the middle of a field, I would most definitely make it back. All of us would make it back. We would figure out a way to get to the next village, or to get clothes, or to make a phone call somewhere. We would figure out a way to get back to reality. It would be a nightmare, but we could do it.

We all have the ability to be street smart buried within us, but it takes a willingness to be that person in order to succeed. You have to decide exactly what you want to do, what you are capable of doing, and if you will follow through when the time comes. I've hired individuals who have lasted less than a week in my office because they were all talk and no business. Once, I had a man working for me who was hired to fly around the world doing trade shows, but he would get so much stage fright before the events that we had to let him go. Eventually, I found someone else who was willing to do it, and she did her job with great ease and professionalism. She loved jumping off a plane in Shanghai to go mix and mingle with strangers.

This lifestyle of high-energy, highly demanding work isn't for everyone. You need to know who you are first before you get out there on the playing field. You will excel once you know who you are, and employers will see that either on your résumé or on your face when you walk in the door. The key to book smarts and street smarts is simply knowing that you are your own best asset. Confidence can be smelled a mile away and felt in the air.

My week is split into sections. Part of the week, I could be at the office working fourteen-hour days, but just as much as I work in the office, I am outside of it, flying around the world to meet with people and build new connections. This is my work, and this is what I'm good at. This is the name of the game when you want to play in the big leagues.

If I were a new hire in an office, I could predict that within the first two to three weeks, there would be a few complaints reported to HR about my work and management style. Working, I have a lot of energy. I'm also aggressive and competitive with my sales tactics. I know this about myself. Rather than toning down my natural skill, I target an environment where I am sure to succeed and lead the crowd, carrying a mission to the end. Flying around the world, meeting new people, and striking up new deals is just my oyster.

I kindly suggest young businesspeople not just get an MBA and look for a job they think they are supposed to have, but rather assess their skills and talents and seek the job they are meant to have and will be successful doing.

The Tom Cruise Effect

If you know yourself and work hard, you will go far. I've been fortunate enough to experience success, and my hope is that you will too. My aspiration is that you will be able to achieve these things without getting cocky or egotistical.

We all know Tom Cruise as a very successful movie star and action hero—an icon. He worked for Paramount Pictures Corporation for over fourteen years and brought in over $14 billion during his tenure. One day, he took the opportunity to go on the *Oprah Winfrey Show*. He sat on her couch and bared his heart, speaking of his work, his trials, and his plans for the future in a way that perhaps not everyone was expecting him to. By the time he climbed off the couch, the CEO of Paramount had fired him, probably thinking he could be easily replaced.

I got to a point in my career where I imagined that I was also irreplaceable. After a track record of closing multimillion-dollar deals and scoring every deal I sought out, I was convinced that I could do anything, go anywhere, and say whatever I wanted to say. If you feed your ego the way I did, you will quickly learn that everyone, even Tom Cruise, is replaceable. There is someone out there who wants your seat on the bench. I was irreplaceable and so was my partner Jamie, a CEO and my mentor … that is, until another company bought our company, and almost as fast as Tom Cruise, we were a part of the past. In the end, no one is indispensible.

CHAPTER 11

Know Your PC

What I want to talk about right now is something I've labeled "PC." When I say "Know your PC," I'm not talking about your computer, although that's a nice way to remember it. Knowing your PC means two things:

1. Know your product.
2. Know your competition.

When I first started working for Terremark, I was shipped across the ocean to make a deal in my home country of Germany. I remember it very clearly, because I was setting up an entire facility. It was my account, so I made every effort to memorize as much about the data center as I could, painting a clear picture of the state-of-the-art facility. This was my baby. It was going to be a big deal for me to make, so I studied every inch of the facility plans. I wanted to know the trail of dollars going into the data center; it helped me understand how we would eventually make the best profit margin.

I worked night and day until I could give tours of the facility in my sleep. Off the top of my head, I was spouting intrinsic knowledge of the work at hand. It was so ingrained in me that the executives I gave tours to would later praise my eloquence. I gave the tours in six languages as needed. I was talking about boring stuff, but I did it with passion and conviction because I'd made it my life. How much did we spend on the infrastructure, the generator, the air-conditioning unit? How much did it cost to build the facility? I knew, therefore I succeeded in my work.

Fast-forward fifteen years. I was no longer with Terremark because it had been bought by Verizon, but I went back as a customer. I was representing a big organization at the time, the Locks Corporation, and I was responsible for taking the CFO to see the former Terremark facility. During the tour, we followed the tour guide, who happened to be the account manager for the company, around the building.

I began to notice that the account manager was giving us a bit of a shallow presentation. On a scale of one to ten, I would assess that his tour could be rated at a six. He was skimping on some of the important information I'd brought my CFO there to learn about.

The account manager didn't know who I was, so I started to ask questions. It was my way of prodding him to give up the goods, to step out of his shell and really sell us on his product. "How much did you spend on the building?" I asked.

"Well, I don't know." He brushed off the question and continued walking.

I shrugged. If he didn't know the answer off the top of his head, I would remind him. "You spent about $125 million on it."

He laughed, truly taken aback. "How do you know?" he asked, the smile on his face bright and beckoning.

"I know," I beamed back, nodding with assurance.

The smile on his face began to crack, but he didn't let it deter him from the tour. He turned on his heel and continued walking toward the next wing of the building. I trailed my CFO, wondering if the guy was going to offer us more information. It was a nice tour, but it was too simple. I really wanted those numbers to impress my CFO, so I called up ahead. "How much did you spend on infrastructure?"

The party came to a halt again as he stopped and turned to face me once more. "I don't know." He smiled and shook his head.

"You spent $86 million," I said with a nod, smiling right back at him. I hoped he'd catch on to what I was doing. Without saying it outright, I needed him to give us the facts.

He chuckled, "You're good. You really know this stuff."

I batted away his politeness, realizing with gravity that this man probably didn't know the information I was trying to get out of him. "How much did you spend for each generator?"

"I'm not sure either," he said, squirming, his smile fading, confirming my suspicion.

"Almost €112,000" was the answer. I decided I wasn't going to stop just because he didn't know. I began to elaborate on my knowledge, letting it pour out of me in narrative form. Suddenly, it was my tour, not his, and we stood there on the last leg of our journey until I had finished informing my CFO of all the information I thought he needed to know at this point.

The guy, silenced by my intellect, looked down at the clipboard in his hands. Flipping from page to page, he asked, "Who are you and where are you from?"

I didn't give him an answer. The tour ended, and we shook hands to leave. Later, the man went back to the office where he brought up the encounter with other Terremark personnel. They confirmed my identity as the guy who brought the rest of the world to the data center. I'm sure he got a laugh out of that himself.

It wasn't my intention to embarrass him, but I think he probably learned a lesson from that encounter and thereafter took the time to really learn the thing he was spending forty to eighty hours a week promoting and talking about. My least favorite thing when dealing with salespeople is running into those who don't know their product. Knowing your PC inside and out enables you to exude confidence while building customer trust in whatever you are selling. Most importantly, it can be the deciding factor in making or breaking any business deal.

Scoop the Competition

In the newspaper world, they have a saying that I like. When one newspaper steals a story from another, it is called "getting the scoop." Their entire business model is built on getting a big story out to the public before competitors can swoop in and feed it to their audiences instead. If a certain newspaper is the last one to find out the facts about a scandal in the White House or the death of a celebrity, it loses credibility, it loses its audience, and then it loses money.

However, getting the scoop doesn't just apply to newspapers. Every business has a rival. Someone out there is looking to take your customers and your dollars from you. When your business is successful, your ultimate goal is to avoid getting scooped. The truth, however, is that everything is bound to be copied. If you churn out a successful product or service, someone is going to replicate it. Imitation is the sincerest form of flattery.

For example, taxis will take you from point A to point B. They've been doing this since the dawn of time. In comes the transport company Uber with the same offerings: they will take you from point A to point B, but they will do it for less money, and they will put you in contact with your driver so that you know precisely when he or she pulls up to your doorstep.

Right now, there is a war raging between common taxi services and Uber. Uber is quite literally scooping taxis right out of business. Uber is genius. With two taps, I have a black car waiting for me outside. However, Uber already has competition. If you haven't heard of Lyft, you will soon, because the company is right on Uber's coattails. This is the way the market works.

You will never be able to keep competitors from cropping up. Your power lies in taking proactive steps to stay on top. Know your PC: your product and your competition. Know what you are selling inside and out so that your competitors won't be able to reach your standard of excellence when they finally do get into the game.

Returning to my PC story above, I visited the data-center facility in Germany with my CFO because I wanted him to see how this company was miles ahead of its competitors, but the account manager was not prepared. He didn't know his product. I wonder if he was aware how close my CFO was to reaching out to his competitor. If he knew what his competitor was doing, he probably would have studied. He would have given us a tour I could rate as a ten rather than a lackluster six.

Now I look back and I know I saved his account that day. When I was in his position, I made sure that if I had a CFO in front of me, I had memorized all the necessary numbers and knew my information. I did it so well that fifteen years later, I still knew those numbers. He, on the other hand, looked at the building from the perspective of a tourist. There was a CFO in front of him who spoke that language of numbers, and he wasn't able to say how much the building was worth.

The second problem was that the account manager did not know how to present the product. My CFO loved the building. He kept pointing out things he was impressed with, yet the account manager was shy on information and slow to deliver relevant facts. In my opinion, the account manager should never have been hired. I will tell you right now, as the customer, I know that building is worth $5 billion. I told my CFO why it was so expensive to build that building so that he could understand more of the billing structure. It made sense to him. The project manager had officially been scooped.

It doesn't really matter what your trade is. You can be a car salesman, a real estate agent, or both. Unless you are a godlike omnipotent being, you will not be able to simply become all-knowing. You will need to study—and study hard. I studied hard and look where it got me. It doesn't matter what you sell, you have to know the product, otherwise, you'll stumble, and it will be apparent.

There is always a silver lining of common sense in every situation. When in doubt, use your common sense. Know your audience, your product, and how to present your product to your audience. These are the relevant, commonsense factors in any sales relationship.

Features of a Great Product

Present your product in such a way that people can understand its value. Sometimes, the value isn't as apparent as you may think. The account manager leading us on the data-center tour was willing to charge my CFO approximately $80 per square foot. This quote was actually a bit higher than other data centers, and my CFO noted that. Instead of going into detail about what my CFO would be getting within that price block, the account manager skipped on to new things. This signaled to both of us that he did not know the pricing breakdown and maybe believed that my CFO was going to sign the deal simply because he had come all that way to check out the facility. What a backward way of thinking. I told my CFO that the original floor plan cost the company $585 per square foot to build—and that was because of the state-of-the-art equipment and infrastructure installed there. These facts served to sell my CFO on the facility.

How do you know if you have a great product? You won't know unless you have the facts, the data representing it. You will know what features of your product to promote when you are actually selling a lot of it. At that time, you will want to figure out a way to promote your product in the simplest fashion. I say this because of experience.

We've all walked into that one store that is jam-packed with products. The walls are covered with items and our senses are destroyed, thinking, "What do I want to buy? What did I come in here for?" These stores don't make it big. Simplicity makes it big.

There is a reason why Apple is one of the largest and most successful businesses in the world. It is so successful because the company has a unique way of featuring the products they know we want. Walk into an Apple store and you will see the array of product displays laid out chicly on pristine white tables. It's so clean and simple that you can't help but walk up to a device and check it out. The brilliance of the store design invites curiosity while answering any subconscious questions you have about value.

I walked into an AT&T store the other day and realized that they had taken a page out of Apple's book. All of their merchandise was splayed out on tables. Personnel wandered the room with tablets asking customers if they needed help. They'd abandoned their walls full of phone cases and boxes packed with chargers for every kind of device, and streamlined their product displays just like Apple.

Maybe you don't have a storefront. Maybe you have a single product or an online service. Whatever it is, simplify the language defining your product. Simplify it in a way that those features just pop for customers. Take a page out of Apple's book. I promise, you won't regret it.

When I present my product, whether it's mutual funds or data centers, I streamline it just like Apple. For instance, you can't buy just an iPhone case or an iPhone car charger. In order to buy product B, you need to first purchase product A. The Apple store is chic because upon entering, you only see product A. The salespeople are hard at work getting you to walk out of the store with product A. Then, and only then, will they try to interest you in products B, C, and D.

Don't pack the shelves, pack the storage space in the back. In an Apple store and now even in an AT&T store, you will decide on a product and the salesperson will walk to the back, go behind a door, and come back out with the item you've purchased.

I want this to be your modus operandi too. Pack your brain full of information for your client, but be prepared to talk about the best features in the simplest form. When they ask for more information, go back to your shelves, whether for relevant data or your team, and retrieve what you need to seal the deal.

I can stand in front of a CTO and make a sale not because I know everything about the tech side, but because I let him or her know I am willing to go get the necessary information. "I'm sorry," I will say if I don't know an answer right off the bat. "I'm not the CTO of the company. Give me all of your questions, and I will have them answered within twenty-four hours."

Creating Repeat Customers

Purchasing power is not exercised in a rational way. Although salespeople present products to consumers as if there is logic in the design of the pricing, we all know that people buy things that meet emotional needs. It is a well-known fact that over 50 percent of the consumer experience is based on emotion. Whether it is a conscious behavior or not, we are all responding to products by how they make us feel. Once a product gains our emotional trust, consumers are more likely to offer loyalty and advocacy in an effort to respond to that churned-up passion.

Passion has a tangible effect on the growth or stagnation of a business. There are plenty of businesses out there that don't make the effort to establish an emotional connection with their consumers. This is a large mistake, because without an emotional stake in the brand, customers will purchase a product or service once and then move on to another, similar brand whenever convenient. There isn't a brand out there that doesn't have a rival. The easiest examples are Coca-Cola versus Pepsi and Verizon versus AT&T. The commonality between all of these brands is that they have established an emotional connection, some could say a relationship, with their consumers. These brands have been very intentional about it too. Yes, they have incredible products, but without the element of human connection, they would not survive. These exceedingly successful brands have found a way to tap into the hearts of their primary customers by influencing, and even assuaging, the emotional connections.

By engaging your customer on an emotional level, you establish a long-term purchasing relationship. This kind of branding takes time and energy. Not only do you have to figure out who your customers are, but you also have to envision what they will respond to emotionally.

Sell the Dream, Not the Reality

We've all seen the million-dollar advertisements aired during the Super Bowl. Those three hours of primetime television include commercials about all of the hottest brands of car, yet each one will have a different tactic for seeking out its customers. Whether it is the power of a Dodge, the prestige of a Mercedes-Benz, or the sex appeal of a Lexus, automobile brands have done their research and know what their target audience will respond to. This is an effort to engage in an emotional dialogue with customers.

Logically, nobody needs a Lexus when there are less expensive cars available, yet the message of emotional belonging is heard far above what is logical. This kind of appeal fosters connectedness, and customers who experience this kind of intense desire for a brand are the ones who will become long-term purchasers. We know for a fact that emotionally engaged customers are less likely to shop around, less interested in basing their purchase on prices, and exceedingly more likely to buy a product again and again as well as share their findings with their friends.

It's all in the power of relationships. Branding empires know that they grow and continue to make money from customers who continue to shop with them. An article by Gallup, Inc. entitled "Customer

Satisfaction Doesn't Count" itemizes the places where customers find worth. Where a customer finds worth, a business finds loyalty and sales. Satisfaction is not enough—customers want more than just something that works. They want something that will sustain them, and Gallup identifies these items as confidence, integrity, pride, and passion. This is what you would expect in a relationship, right?

In order to ensure that customers perceive these qualities in whatever brand I am representing, I've learned to put the customer at the base of everything I do. After all, the customer is the person who is signing my checks, paying my mortgage, and enabling me to eat every day. The customer has all of my attention, and I want to empathize with that individual, which later leads to relationship building.

Building customer loyalty is very close to the process of building relationships. In previous chapters, I discussed the ways relationships penetrate deeper than a résumé. Who you know often trumps what you know, and we can't let that logic escape us here. Customers are looking for a relationship, so I offer that by putting them first on my list.

Building relationships means being empathetic and putting yourself in the shoes of the customer. If I were the customer, how would I feel about the services I'd paid for? How would I respond after using this product? The point of asking these questions is to step into the mind of the consumer. It is the same tactic I use when approaching executives I want to partner with. I ask myself, "How can I get closer to them and really offer something they will feel a connection to?"

Empathy Creates Loyalty

Empathy can go a long way. I don't know if you spend much time in supermarkets or coffee shops. You may not, but here's something I've found upon entering Whole Foods Market, Starbucks, and Jamba Juice: these brands have found a way to enrich the point-of-sale experience by giving employees the customer experience as well as creating a lifestyle. Salespeople standing at Starbucks registers can talk about anything during that short transaction—they can talk about the weather or they can talk about Starbucks products. Starbucks, I'm certain, would prefer that their employees talk about purchase items. That is why they give employees free samples of the products. Each employee is allowed to take a pound of coffee or tea home each week. This engrosses them in the brand and turns them into experts on the floor. By allowing salespeople to experience Starbucks products for free, they provide a conversation starter for times when customers ask them about products.

I'm sure you've heard this dialogue in a Starbucks:

"Is this new juice good?"

"Absolutely, I've tried it and love it. My favorite is …"

The emotional connection has been established because the salesperson can empathize with the desire of the customer. A bond has been created, and the customer will more than likely try the item the salesperson suggested. Personal encounters and likeability sell products.

Conversations vs. Presentations

Jamie wasn't my only partner on business trips when I worked with Terremark. I used to work alongside other sales reps on their accounts. One trip in particular sticks out in my mind. It is the perfect example of how personable customers should expect salespeople to be. As you're reading this, think of it on a more global scale than the boardroom. You can draw similar parallels between this and the sales floor, or even the task of getting yourself a new deal. It's always important to know when you should put away the slides and engage your audience one-on-one.

Have you ever been in a meeting where the presenter has made an art show of their PowerPoint slides? They have all the bells and whistles—moving animation, a strategic color scheme, and so many slides you wonder if they've considered writing a book. It can be exciting at first, but once you've sat through the first hour, or maybe even the first fifteen minutes, you are so inundated with information that you're ready to fall asleep. Even the most disciplined among us will start to wonder what else is going on in the world. You check your phone, you lose focus, and finally, you zone out.

It is the knowledgeable salesperson who relies on slides as a tool who will be able to make a deal in a hot tub, on an elevator door, at a steakhouse, or on the hoods of cars because he or she has a deep and intrinsic understanding of what he or she is selling. My hope for you is that you will take the time to really study every inch of your business so that when the customer asks you a question, you will know your facts so well that they come out in a casual, convincing tone. I believe in conversations over presentations because it's been my observation that many business professionals use presentations as a crutch.

To illustrate this, I recall once working closely with the account executive for MFS Networks. Sally and I needed to seal the deal on her MFS account. Our next step was to fly to White Plains, New York, to persuade a group of executives that our products and services were the best for their business. Unbeknownst to me, Sally brought a projector with her on the plane and proceeded to set it up in the boardroom. The twelve or so executives settled themselves in for a presentation. After making our acquaintances, Sally walked to the far window and closed the blinds. With the exception of the projector's illuminating glow, we were in total movie-theater darkness. Sally turned her back to the group and began reading through her presentation.

Within the first three minutes, small conversations began to crop up around the room. The chatter grew into a steady mumble, and then phone screens began to light up the darkness. Sally had lost them. I sat in the back and watched it all unfold. I wasn't feeling too well—not because of what was happening but because I was actually exhausted from a bad headache that I couldn't shake. I thought about what would happen if I sat back and nodded off in the presentation. I surveyed the room once more, weighed my options, and realized this just wasn't going to work. I looked over at my CEO with the intent of communicating my concern, but even she was getting that glazed-over look.

That's one of the traps of the PowerPoint presentation. It is such an efficient way to display book loads of information that we forget it's designed to be an aid, not the main focus. The line dividing those two things is very thin, which is why my CEO didn't pick up on the concerned look I shot her. If I didn't do something quickly, the room was going to fall asleep, and we would have made the trip for absolutely nothing.

"You know what, Sally—before we get into that, we should talk about something else first."

Heads in the room snapped in my direction as I stood from my seat. I walked over to the blinds and pulled them back, turning to see eyes squinting into the wash of light entering the room.

"I want to know a bit about these guys before we get into your presentation. Is that okay?"

Honestly, what was Sally to do? I had more authority within the organization, and we both knew that the question was just to be polite. I was rescuing the meeting from her dreary slideshow. Sally relented and sat in her seat, maybe a little relieved for the moment that she didn't have to force her way through another presentation. I stopped the projector and went to the board. With a red marker, I drew a map of the United States with our data centers blinking out in black and blue, and then I wheeled around to see who was watching me. The room was silent; the executives had abandoned their BlackBerry phones and were gawking at me quizzically.

I returned their gaze evenly, with no idea of what I would pull out of my hat. Here I'd made this grand gesture to put the train back on its tracks, but I didn't have any slides of my own. I didn't have a planned presentation, only the meeting agenda. I had to do something to create a conversation, to draw the conversation to me and what I had to offer them—which was 7,500 square feet of data-center space, so that's what I led with. I started a conversation with them, asking them what they needed and wanted. I asked them how we could help to fix some of the problems they were facing.

I then went through the agenda, and it was by the grace of conversation and the naturally humanistic desire to relate that the meeting got off the ground. In the end, it didn't just get off the ground— we received the green light from the CCO. After conferring with legal, we closed a multimillion-dollar deal.

At the end of the day, my CEO approached me. "You know, Ben, had you not done that, we would have lost everything."

There are a few lessons to learn here, and again, I hope you can apply them globally to the tasks you will tackle and the field you work in. In my experience, I've learned that about 80 percent of my customers prefer to have a conversation over viewing a presentation. I am not very good at creating presentations and will be the first one to admit it. However, I am very good at presenting at meetings. It's not that I couldn't pull a presentation together if prompted; it's that I don't believe in them. So I am not motivated to create them.

My belief is that the artful PowerPoint is a crutch for weak salespeople to lean on. It may sound harsh, but I'm not here to lie to you. A good presentation that includes PowerPoint will allot twelve to seventeen minutes for the slides; the rest of the time will be devoted to actually presenting, which consists of conversation and fact sharing. My presentations typically focus on two or three main pages which I use as a visual reference tool for the audience. The slides are for the audience, not for me. Most of the time, I end up turning the presentation into a conversation anyway. I let my customers ask me questions, and I take the time to go over the responses in detail.

I'm not suggesting that people shouldn't be prepared. I'm saying that they shouldn't have to rely on the information they've packed into their PowerPoints. The all-knowing salesperson will have all of the information stored in his or her head.

I once gave a lecture where the students had to compare and contrast the marketing between Chrysler and Fiat. The group succeeded because individually, they each knew more about their persuasive arguments and data than what was reflected in the PowerPoint. I liked this. Next, I coached them on how to have a conversation while leaning on the facts that they knew. From that day, my students learned how to seek out what the audience or listeners were interested in and then to tie those interests back into the items they were selling or the information they were peddling.

The second thing I taught my students was the power of a story. Some of the student presenters thought it was a good idea to stand up there and read the slides to the class. I know where the desire to do this comes from—a lack of preparation. Don't read your audience your slides. Just because you are saying it out loud doesn't mean that it will be any more appealing. Story is appealing. While your audience is sifting through the information on your screen, summarize what's there in a story. Stories have the power to create interest. They get the mind going and suddenly, the dry information your audience is reading is applicable to their lives.

This way of presenting holds true to every audience. Financial executives are usually the exception. Anything to do with financials should be presented on a single page, printed out and handed to attendees. It should be a fast-fact sheet, not a twenty-nine-slide PowerPoint presentation. The fast-fact sheet should be an overview of the return on investment, the story of the company, and bullet points on why choosing your company makes sense.

So, remember your PC: know your product, know your competition. And exhibit customer empathy while selling the dream, not the reality. Presentations can be useful tools to have in your arsenal, but they are not a substitute for the organic process of meaningful conversations with your prospects and customers.

CHAPTER 12

The Self-Discipline of Sales Calls

Becoming an effective leader in any business requires stamina and dedication to the task. Would my journey have been more bearable if I'd had a map? Maybe so. Maybe some pylons, roadblocks, and neon signs pointing me in the right direction would have done me good, but I didn't have that. I wish I'd had all the answers at age twenty-six. I spent so much time blazing my own trail. That's part of the reason I have been so successful. But I truly would have benefited from someone writing down the information for me.

The lessons I learned were all learned from firsthand experience. I'm honored to have the opportunity to write them here for you, yet as a reader, you must know that the advice I offer is nothing more than advice. If you don't get out there and apply it while pushing yourself to your own limits, it's nothing more than words on paper.

Something I discovered during my first months as a salesman in Germany, and then again at Terremark with Jamie, was that I truly was my own best asset. I had to treat every customer as if he or she signed my paycheck. I needed to be aggressive, take calculated risks, and realize the hard way that the road to success is often riddled with potholes. I spent my twenties learning that as well as how to read and talk to people. As I grew older, I made fewer mistakes, and my business grew. However, if it weren't for those first formative years of pushing myself to my absolute limits, I wouldn't be here today to tell you my story.

Wealth, prestige, passion—these are all reasons why we work hard at our jobs. Take a peek into my life, and you will see that I have a lot of these things. I like toys, and I have a few very fun ones to play with. I drive nice cars, I live in a wealthy neighborhood, I wear designer clothes, and I fly first class around the world. Isn't this the American dream? I think that many of us have forgotten that the American dream also includes years and years of hard work. Sometimes that hard work doesn't amount to wealth, just access to fulfillment and a good life. Working hard at the thing that you love should afford you your own personal form of happiness.

When I first started at Terremark with Jamie, I worked two entire years without a vacation, much less a day off. There wasn't an option to take a break. I worked tirelessly long hours alongside Jamie and our CEO. I think the closest I got to a vacation was having work meetings in places where people often took vacations. I can't tell you how many times I've been to Hawaii. People go there to get away—I went to sit through lengthy meetings and sign documents. I never spent a day on the beach or ventured much farther than the lobby of my hotel.

I was so close to paradise but never able to take part in it, because I couldn't take myself out of the business. I needed to keep working. Whenever people asked me where I was headed, I would name an exotic location only to see their faces light up.

"Oh, you are spending time in Madrid? I've always wanted to go there."

I laughed because my reply should have been, "Yes, me too!" Someday I would love to visit Madrid and walk around the city as a tourist. Yes, I can do that now, but when my company was just starting, I wasn't able to. I put in all my chips, I put in my time, and my hard work paid off.

How fortunate that I had a partner whose work ethic was identical to mine. Jamie and I would spend days in cities around the world, hammering out the particulars of a deal. Then we would climb aboard the plane for an eight-hour flight back home. Those hours on the plane were precious. We spent every single one working, so that when we landed, we were able to tend to business that had built up in our offices while we were away. After those initial two years, I finally did get a vacation, but my responsibilities to the company only grew. I became the most traveled member of our group.

You're reading this and you may be cringing inside. Where was my time for fun? When did I let go and relax? How did I stay sane? The people who are highly successful are those who take their talent and passion and apply it day in and day out until they have a winning product. That's exactly what I did alongside Jamie. I got in earlier, I stayed later, and I was driven to do more than was expected of me every single day.

If you really want to build something, you have to go all-in, you have to commit. I like to say that if you want to win a car race, you've got to rip out the brakes and just go. In order to have that kind of work ethic, you have to be able to exercise self-discipline.

I think the most accurate definition of self-discipline is the concept of delaying self-gratification in order to achieve an articulated goal. It is difficult to wake up every morning and say, "Okay, I need to make 180 phone calls." Out of those 180 phone calls, you will probably make eighteen real connections. From there, you will probably get five to ten solid sales. At the start of a business, the hours you dedicate are important hours. You may be able wake up the first day and make those 180 calls, but the problem that we all run into is endurance.

A sprinter can wake up one morning and run a mile in seven minutes very easily, especially one who is healthy and agile. I don't know about you, but whenever I start a new hobby, I'm always very excited about it the first time I try it. As an ambitious guy, I may set impossible goals for myself to continue pursuing that hobby. But look at it this way: that sprinter can run a seven-minute mile for two, three, even five miles, but after that will retire into exhaustion. What if that sprinter tries to make the same attempt the next day and the next? How much smarter would it be for sprinters to set a goal in miles and then pace themselves to achieve that goal in minutes? Runners who do not pace themselves will become exhausted and eventually give up the task.

I know that I must pursue my hobbies in moderation, setting healthy goals for myself and giving myself breaks and rewards for the tasks I accomplish. Sometimes, the reward is as small as acknowledging that I completed the task in the first place. We all work such long days; our successes often go unnoticed. The key to self-discipline is not only self-sacrifice but also knowing when to pat yourself on the back for a job well done. To endure the monotony of making 180 calls a day for five days a week, you have to do the following:

- Know yourself.
- Establish a routine.
- Make it personal.

Knowing what kind of business or salesperson you are will help you to complete your task list every day. If you know that you are a morning person, use that to your advantage. Spend the early hours of your day producing your best work. Try not to spend prime hours in a meeting or on a plane. Save those obligations for the second half of your day when you are more prone to daydreaming or in need of a good stretch. The same goes for people who are slow in the morning and faster in the evening. Know your strengths and weaknesses and rely on your teammates to fill in the gaps.

When I know myself, I am able to set a routine. Once I've built my routine, I know what the structure of my day is, and I am less likely to negotiate whether I will do the work or not. I will be less tempted to step out for a long lunch, spend time online shopping, or hover around the break room chatting. Thanks to my routine, I know I am going to do it, so my work entails gearing myself up and preparing to hammer it out.

I approach my routine as if it is my own personal government. My routine defines my day and allows me to make quick decisions about how I use my time. Some people shy away from routines because they feel confining, but I have found that when I allow the work to become personal, I am far more able to concentrate on the task at hand. When my work is close to my heart, I am less likely to abandon things when they become hard. I become aggressive and tactical in my advances to overcome obstacles in my day. When work becomes personal, I become creative, and that's when the fun begins.

If you are a company employee and you want to go far, you have to act as if you are the one running the company. Imagine you are employed by Terremark, as I was. The company pays your salary, but the moment you decide to coast, sit back, and assume those biweekly paychecks are going to keep coming even when you don't perform at the top of your game, that's the moment you've fallen out of love with your work. By taking on the mentality of "I don't need to perform," you've essentially decided to stare at the clock in hopes that the minutes tick by quicker and nobody notices that you're not producing real work. That kind of person may be able to hang around a few years in another department, but the moment you start acting like that in sales, you can assume you'll be let go. At least, if you were in my office, I would fire you.

If I've hired you, then I expect you to be the guy who sees that the race is never over, because he or she hasn't reached the top yet. I want people who act like each of their new acquisitions is a customer in a company they own because the company is not only their livelihood but their passion.

I was self-disciplined because I made the decision to be. When Terremark really took off, I was asked by the HR department to take certain salespeople under my wing and coach them into the kind of people who performed as aggressively as I did on the job. My response? I just didn't see the point. Yes, I could sit down with them and create a performance plan. I could let them tag along with me during the day and be open to their constant questions when they were on their own accounts. Yes, I could do all of those things, but I never saw the point.

If you've been working in any industry for ninety days and you can't find the passion to get up, get out, and go to trade shows to make those sales, then I don't see what anyone can teach you. That kind of passion doesn't come from a coach or a manual, it comes from knowing the importance of your role in your work. You need to nix the mind-set that you are safe and replace it with the notion that you are working for yourself.

I keep telling people to work for themselves, and I feel I need to drive that point home. As larger companies were in play to buy

Terremark, I made the decision to start my own company. Once the acquisition took place, Jamie stayed to transition the company after the sale and eventually started another company, just as I did. I've said that before, but what I didn't say was that many of my clients followed me. Why did they have that kind of reaction when I decided to become an entrepreneur and start my own company? They were more interested in me and the work I had done for them than in Terremark, because I treated the company as if it were mine and them as if they were my very own customers. I answered their calls when I was off the clock. I went out of my way to accommodate special requests. I knew what their kids were doing and where they went on vacation that year. In a way, we shared parts of our lives together, and on that merit they decided to follow me into unknown territory.

If that discipline isn't there for you, then this book won't help to spark that flame. I should be preaching to the choir at this point, not a new convert. Again, you have to be the hustler. You have to step up to the plate, knowing yourself, relying on your routine, and making those 180 phone calls.

Self-Organization

Only you know the best way to organize your time. If the idea of waking up and making 180 calls a day is daunting, then I'll go a step further and explain to you just what I do in order to succeed from task to task. After all, I've expressed that I was the most traveled executive at Terremark. I was the guy who had several meetings a day in different cities around the world. My expense account was double and triple that of other executives. It's one thing to keep your schedule organized, and I had help with that thanks to my assistant; it's quite another to keep yourself organized throughout the day.

In order to succeed at this while keeping myself motivated, I came up with a system of units that I applied to every task. I assigned a block or unit to each task that I needed to get through during my day. Tasks could be as small as getting to a meeting on time or as large as making eighteen calls within the next hour. At the start of my day, I knew how many units I would need to tackle in order for the day to be a success.

Some may say this seems tedious, but the truth remains that when you can visualize your day before it happens, you are more likely to succeed at it. The night before or the morning of, I itemized my daily tasks into units and attacked them one at a time. For instance, Monday morning my first unit was to get to the office by nine a.m. Once there, I knew that I had completed something in my day. Yes, this was a small task, but knowing that it was a goal that I had set and met gave me a little mental boost. Later on in the day, I had to fly to Brazil because I had meetings in Rio de Janeiro. When sitting at my desk making calls and organizing meetings with my assistant, it was easy to get overwhelmed by the fact that I would be stuck on a plane for the next seven hours flying to Rio to meet with people I didn't know. Making these daunting tasks into mere units enabled me to take a bit of the edge off.

Leaving the office and getting to the airport in a timely fashion was my next unit. Checking into the flight, securing a car, attending the meetings, and doing the things I had to do in order to maintain work relationships or create new ones were all separate units. My life became easier because I was getting self-gratification from checking units off my list. In order to be successful, I couldn't miss any units. Every time I looked at my agenda or calendar, I saw the units that I'd completed and the ones I needed to check off.

Things became a bit more complicated when I was traveling between time zones. We are all governed by time, and it can be mentally and physically disorienting to find yourself in five time zones within the same week and deal with the jet lag that follows. You really have to know your body and be able to sleep when the sun is still up. In order to stay on task, I learned to work in my time zone from home and didn't change the time on my wristwatch or computer when traveling to other countries. I found that if I ignored the sun and the habits of the people around me—eating, sleeping, working—and behaved as if I were in my home city, then I stayed on task and kept my sanity.

Whatever your system is, you need to let it govern your life so that you are not making unnecessary decisions during the day. Let your system be your religion and stick to it regardless. And of course, make sure it works for you, not against you.

Being organized and using my units was important because it helped me to keep abreast of what was changing from location to location. The only tangible thing we have in our lives is time, and time was the thing giving me energy. I would look at my schedule and see I had a hundred units for the week. I could easily note that I'd completed sixty of them and had forty yet to go. It was gratifying to see all the work I had accomplished. It inspired me to tackle the rest of it, like a distance runner.

Example of Units	Unit	Complete
Taxi ride	11	
Check-in/fly	12	
Landing/customs	13	
Taxi ride to hotel	14	
Hotel check-in	15	
Taxi ride to meeting location	16	
Conduct meeting	17	

Global Accounts Management

Global account management has become necessary in part due to the Internet. Companies like IBM and Xerox were the first to truly utilize their global market, creating IT services that were comparable and compatible in markets around the globe. The fact that there are so many companies with multinational customers furthers the need for global account managers. Having been one, I can tell you that it's not an easy job, and it's definitely not for everyone.

In order to get the job I did, you will have to go through grueling interviews and have knowledge of global accounts. If you want to get to a place where you are being considered for a global account management position, you have to get comfortable with sales and with flying around the world. My rules for salespeople are the same as for global account managers:

- You cannot make deals in your office.
- The only office you have is the tray table in the airplane.
- The 80/20 rule reigns supreme, so be in the 20 percent of salespeople who succeed, not the 80 percent who fail.

You see, when a company hires you, they are not just compensating you for your time; they are paying for far more than salary. The bill includes expenses you will accrue on business trips—everything from ransom insurance to cabs, flights, and dinners with clients. Because of this expense, you are going to have to have an interview with every single person on the executive team before anyone gives you a job. It's a grueling process, but this is an investment for them. The expectation of the board will be that you know how to manage your time and won't crumble under the pressure when there is a high demand for your attention.

When you have a global territory like I did, you will need to conduct five to ten meetings every ten days. This will cost the company about $20,000. That's roughly $2,000 per meeting. The miles you fly will have a direct impact on your sales numbers, your quota, and your compensation. The year I flew around the world, my salary was phenomenal. Last year, it wasn't in the same ballpark, but that's because I wasn't flying nearly as often. That is an incentive for you to get out there and make sales. My former boss, Frank Demmer, the one who got me started in Germany, had a strict rule about being in the office. If he found anyone at a desk between the hours of nine o'clock in the morning and six o'clock at night, he would take the items on their desks and throw them out of the window.

We Germans are an intense bunch when it comes to business. Frank's actions may seem extreme to some cultures, but in the field we were in, we had to take it in stride. I never threw any of my salespeople's items out of the window, but I sure wished I could have sometimes. Your office has to be on the plane or in the customers' offices. You can't sign deals in your office or over the phone. You have to do it face-to-face with your customer.

Of all company sales, 80 percent will be made by 20 percent of the sales team. That means that 80 percent of the team will be sitting at their desks waiting for you to make the next deal so that they can get a paycheck. Promise me that you will be in the 20 percent. Manage your time like it's a budget. Maintain a fine balance between your work life and your personal life. Be personable to your customers. Try to get everything in during one meeting. Be organized, because you are spending the company's dollars.

I was flying to New York one week with Jamie because we were notified of an account manager who was abusing his expense card. He decided to fly into New York on the company's dime not because he had a meeting, but because he wanted to see his girlfriend who was living there. I was flabbergasted when I found out. How could he use company money to do a thing like that? Jamie and I were disheartened to discover that he was using company dollars to fund other excursions as well. Needless to say, he was fired. It's important for the team to see there is zero tolerance for dishonesty or a lack of representation, a clear example of violating the company's code of ethics; we will always protect our brand. As an account manager, you will be gifted with many responsibilities on the merit of your integrity. I can't remember a single time when I made the decision to sit back on my haunches and take the company's time and money for granted.

The closest I ever got to abusing my company card was a time in Rio de Janeiro when immigration went on strike. For the entire day, there were absolutely no flights in or out of Brazil. Part of being emotionally intelligent and organized is knowing when to throw in the towel. I took the hint, retired my computer to my hotel room in exchange for beachwear, and headed out to find myself some sun. I sat on the beach for two days instead of standing in the airport, waiting for things to change. The immigration problem was eventually resolved, and I was free to return to my work. So unless you are stranded in paradise in the middle of an immigration strike, there is no good reason to do what that gentleman did in New York.

You Are Your Best Asset

I had the opportunity to buy my house from a gentlemen who became a developer after a very successful career that left him a millionaire. Two years after I bought my house from him, I was flying from Atlanta to Miami when I noticed that someone on the plane had the same demeanor as the man who sold me my house.

"Henry? Is that you?" I asked.

The man across the aisle peeled his reading glasses down the bridge of his nose to look over at me.

My grin was bright and friendly. "What are you doing here?" We both sat in business class seats, which surprised me.

Henry, recognizing me, grinned back. Leaning over the aisle, he shook my hand warmly. "Hello, Ben, it's good to see you again."

"What are you doing here?" I asked again. "You're a millionaire a couple times over. Shouldn't you be on your own private jet?"

The smile faded slightly and was replaced with a stern look. He shook his head, "No, Ben, I am working."

I didn't get it. "What do you mean, you are working? You own businesses—you hire people to fly around the world and do this stuff for you."

"No," he said, frowning. He reached to his face and took his glasses off. "Never ever, ever."

"You've got me baited. I need to know why." The last time I saw him he was leaving my newly bought house to go play golf with his son.

Henry indulged me and laid it out, explaining that he once had a very productive business. He sold plants and flowers and only had two big accounts: Home Depot and Walmart. He was the only supplier they bought from, and he supplied plants for every single one of their stores nationwide. He expressed that he guarded those relationships closely. Personally, I understood this. As a linguist, I have relationships with foreign telecom companies simply because I speak their language: Telecom Italia, Telefonica, Deutsche Telekom, and others are companies that know me very well. I only need a few strong relationships to make them powerful accounts for my business.

"Yes, I understand that." I gave him my examples, and he nodded along politely.

"But do you want to know why I don't hire people and put them on my accounts?" Henry asked.

Henry owned his business for many years and grew weary of flying around the country to attend meetings. They were only two accounts, but they kept him busy. Being busy meant that he was constantly away from his family. As his kids grew up, he realized he was missing out on their lives. When the time came, he decided to sell his business. He sold it for $48 million and retired to work as a real estate agent/developer. That is how I met him, and he was still doing very well for himself as a developer. He still got to travel, and above all else, he was able to spend ample time with his kids and his wife.

Two years later, he was approached by the now heads of the company he sold. They came knocking on his door asking him to buy the company back. After two years, they had run it into the ground. Henry agreed to buy it back. After all, it was his baby. But he didn't do it for the price he sold it at. He picked it back up for ten cents to the dollar because they'd run his pristine business through the mud. Within one year, he was producing $60 million in revenue and flying back every week to attend to his two accounts.

"But you have four children," I said. "Why not make them do it?"

"No discipline." He pushed his glasses back onto his face. "Instead, I bought an air pass."

From this lesson, I hope you gather the truth about the business world. It is by your own hand and self-discipline that you will succeed in sales, not by coasting on the coattails of others who have worked hard.

CHAPTER 13

Developing an Advisory Board

I have spoken about emotional intelligence and fostering different types of business relationships throughout the book. Now I'll introduce you to what is arguably the most important relationship you will develop: the C-level connection. While interfacing with your colleagues, working with customers, and training your teams are key, maintaining close relationships with C-level executives in your industry and building high-level networks are critical to actually enabling the business to get done, the deal to go through.

When I started BVS Consulting, initially I needed help. All of us do when we launch a new business. In the beginning, I looked to friends, colleagues, and even former clients to support my new endeavor.

It's very easy to get an idea for a company. You may even go so far as to launch it on your own while following your instinct. But unless you've taken the time to vet your ideas and really let them germinate and grow, your company will remain flat, one-dimensional, and ultimately unsuccessful. If you want your business to be as successful as a lemonade stand, then ignore this next chapter. The key is to keep the momentum going when following your dream.

As I said before, I initially reached out to people I knew in the business world who were willing to give me honest feedback. The job started with dinners out, with phone calls and invitations to sit and talk. Those who were able to hear me out in earnest and even offer constructive criticism were the people I eventually asked to be part of my advisory team. I did this with the open invitation that I would eventually ask them to be on my board of directors.

When choosing who will be your eyes and ears as you start to build your infant idea into a strong, mature business venture, you must first find the right players. The right players will offer the following:

- a network they are comfortable sharing with you
- skill as problem solvers and solution seekers
- support for your good ideas and challenges for your questionable ones
- honesty about the amount of time they can offer you and what they are expecting in return for their efforts

I can't say it enough that when you step out of your door in the morning, you should approach any sales task with passion, determination, and intention. Organizing an advisory team is exactly that—a sales pitch. If at any time you are unsure of why you are starting your business or portray that you are not 100 percent invested in your work, whoever you are propositioning to be on your team will sense the hesitation. Even if you are unsure of the particulars of your business, you are still in control.

It will help to know what you intend your advisory board to help you with. Yes, they will be your eyes and ears as you embark on this exciting new journey, but you are still the leader and decision maker. You are the one with the innate passion, not them. Be sure to remain in the leadership position and instruct them on what they should be looking and listening for. This means having your agenda ready when they arrive. Just like any meeting, make sure your team knows what you will be entertaining and discussing before they get there, especially if it is a meaty and complicated subject. They will appreciate your thoughtfulness in preparing them.

Furthermore, I would also highly suggest requiring your advisory team's full confidentiality accompanied by a simple written agreement. In return, you should be prepared to compensate them, especially as they transition into board members. Consider that if someone were to approach you and ask for your time, networks, and the kind of advice that has taken you an entire career to glean, wouldn't you expect something in return? Even if that person is your dear friend or an acquaintance, you would still expect more than a simple thank-you.

It is not uncommon to compensate your advisory team with paid meals whenever you meet or even travel expenses when they are asked to join you somewhere. You may consider giving them a percentage of your company, stock options, or everyone's favorite, cash. Whomever you choose to be on your team will also gain connections they didn't have before. They will have access to your networks, to new ideas and changes in the market. The benefits vary, so don't sell yourself short. The key is to build a cohesive team to generate consensus.

Remember that it's your show, but you should remain open to receiving the best advice. You will also need to make sure that everyone who shows up is actually contributing to your project and on the same page as you. If at any time you notice someone on your advisory team becoming complacent, conflictive, unresponsive, or constantly lagging at meetings, you should ask that person to refocus and/or retire. The advisory team members will begin to show their true colors after a few meetings, and you will be able to separate the wheat from the chaff. Those who've decided to invest in your dream will demonstrate so in word and in action. Those are the heavyweights you want to approach and ask to be board members in the long run. At least, that's the way I would do it. Surround yourself with talented and smart people who can contribute as members of the big league.

Executive-Team Qualities

Ultimately, it is through the references of my board members and their networks that I find people to interview for my executive team. Everyone from my COO to my CFO will need to have the following qualities:

- effective communication skills
- a balance of book smarts and street smarts

- self-confidence but with an awareness of personal limits and a willingness to seek help when necessary
- an ability to make hard decisions in business and invite feedback from people
- great passion for his or her work
- a maniacal customer focus that views the customer as the employer
- a knowledge of how to take the small "yes" and then quickly move on to work for a hard "yes"
- an instinctive drive for closure and the skill to secure the final contract

This may look like a tall order, but in demanding excellence from my team, I enable myself to fully depend on them for the continued survival of my company.

Ups and Downs of Networking

Establishing relationships with and building vast networks of C-level professionals is key to business success. It's all about who you know. I will use the networks of my advisory board because connections in any industry all run together. Worldwide, we have six degrees of separation. In the telecom industry, there are two or three degrees of separation. Maintaining your networks is an important responsibility.

I was once working on a contract in Madrid when I got a call from my assistant. "Ben, I've been trying to reach you, where have you been? Where is Jamie?" My secretary knows that if I'm abroad, it may be more difficult to reach me, but she was insistently calling, so I knew something was up.

She began to tell me about a tour that had been conducted in our flagship data center. A data-center representative, we'll call him George, was giving a client a tour. As the client was taken around the facility, he appeared unimpressed by the state-of-the-art equipment and merely grunted as George took him from room to room. The client showed so little interest that George began to get angry, although he kept his cool until the end of the tour. He asked the client outright what he was impressed with, and the client still had nothing positive to say.

This would have frustrated me as well, as I knew that our data center was really something that we had engineered with brilliance. It was truly the Rolls-Royce of the industry at that time. It was the first of its kind, and we were so proud of it that we couldn't imagine someone in our field not being excited or impressed after realizing its potential. However, this client remained unimpressed, and when George asked him, "How did you like it?" the man replied flatly, "It was all right."

George was not a hotheaded guy, but he definitely felt slighted and cursed under his breath. Typically, the meeting would have ended there, with the client sulking off to his hotel room. But the client came back with a vengeance and made it known to George that the telecom world is very small.

"You know what?" the client retaliated. "I am going to make sure no one in this industry ever steps foot into this facility again."

In retrospect, if I had been in the meeting, that never would have happened. If ever I see that individuals don't immediately connect in a conducive way for the meeting to continue, I find a way to get the troublemaker out of the way so we can reach our goal and sign a contract. If I had been there, I would have seen that he didn't connect right off the bat, and I would have escorted our data-center representative out of the meeting. It would have saved his job, and it would have saved us the headache.

The client left, and before he even reached the parking lot, he had a multinational telecommunications company on the phone telling their executive leadership not to work with us. Moreover, the client called every single executive at another leading telecommunications and Internet service provider. He went on down his speed dial list, calling everyone with the intent to blackball us because our data-center representative, George, lost his cool and insulted him.

My assistant had my ear now. She was beckoning me to come back to the United States so we could fix this big mess. I was in the middle of closing my own big deal, so traveling right away was out of the question. First things first: of course, George had to be fired. Instead of spending eight hours on a plane, Jamie and I set to work repairing every single one of those relationships that took us years to build in order to get our business back on track.

I ran up a bill of $10,000 in Madrid doing damage control thanks to roaming charges, but we had to convince people that errors happen and that our data-center representative had a bad day. Eventually, we had to fly to the client and hold meetings with the company's executives to backpedal and fix everything that happened. It took me two years to close the original deal because of that mishap. Now you know how powerful maintaining networks and relationships can be.

The Wrench in the Works

When you have a well-established business and start to lose customers, it may not be because your product is inferior—it may be because of people like George and their inability to give your customers what they want. The problems that happen between customers and a business can all come to a head with the salesperson. That person is in direct contact with what the customer wants, and through his or her actions, the company you've built with your own two hands can either succeed or fail in a matter of seconds.

You may think this is a bit dramatic, but here lies the truth: when you discover a wrench in the works, nothing will fix it like an intelligent person willing to get his or her hands dirty. Intelligence wins wars. Your business will survive to see another day if you use intelligence and practicality to solve the problem.

We've all seen it: a situation in which one person neglects to enter a customer complaint correctly and suddenly you are losing business. For whatever reason, no one is addressing the customer's concern. That single customer is representative of hundreds more who are facing the same problem that the company is failing to solve, all because one employee failed to enter data, follow through with a promise, talk to another department, or even see the light.

At first it is a very small, manageable problem. In large companies, these small wrenches can be passed around the office for a while. One manager doesn't want to take responsibility for the issue, so he or she points fingers at another department. From there, the problem is passed around again and again until it is actually a much larger problem than when it originated. Why are customers unhappy with your service? Your war is now to find out where the wrench is and remove it, not just pass the buck.

If strategy is the big picture, then competitive analysis is the act of taking apart and figuring out what is wrong with the machine itself. Using competitive analysis to solve a problem is the work of turning your attention to the details in order to follow the bread-crumb path back to where the problem originated. I always did my own due diligence. I looked at the whole picture first, and then I focused in on problem areas until the original flaw was discovered.

I worked alongside a lot of managers on these internal issues who had no sense of responsibility for their mistakes. As a CEO or COO, when you run an organization you cannot turn a blind eye to the war of business and competition. If you do, then nobody wins, and your company goes down in flames. The best thing you can do is rely on your team. Together, you get your homework done, you make everyone accountable. You correct those mistakes and create consensus to celebrate both short- and long-term wins.

There is no room for excuses. I run into that a lot. Salespeople like George always have an excuse for why they aren't successful. My response is that I don't care. Go fix it. By holding employees accountable for their mistakes, you are simply requiring them to review their work.

"We are getting cancellations" is a term I might hear from my team. In this case, as intelligent human beings and professionals, we sit down together and ask questions like "What will it take to fix this?" Together, we figure it out. This commonsense approach is the most intelligent thing you can do to arrive at a solution. With this question, you will work backward, building confidence in your team and the client, and soon win the war—or at least stand to fight another day.

CHAPTER 14

Studying the Competition

It doesn't matter what industry you are in, you will need to do homework on your competitors before you get started. Every business plan needs information on competitors. Whether it's an internal document or one that others will get the chance to see, working a competitive analysis into your marketing plan, business plan, or prospectus will further your vision and establish your goals. But don't stop there. Take on the game to benefit you at the end! Become the company that updates its analysis annually to reflect the growing trends in your business. Catching trends in the marketplace will help you to know the landscape with each new season.

When I first began my business, I changed my marketing plan once every quarter. Things were moving so fast that I was constantly analyzing the layout of the market, our achievements, and the successes of our competitors. I would hire sales consultants with a single goal at the beginning of a quarter, only to let them go at the end of the quarter if they did not meet their assigned quotas. When that goal shifted and they proved themselves relevant to achieving our goals, they were kept on board. I did this to remain on top of my game, and eventually— through that lens of analysis—my company stabilized and we were able to stand in the market as a real threat to our competitors.

Completing your competitive analysis will start with the work of identifying any business that offers the same product as you do. If you are a start-up, as I was, don't get caught up in how far ahead in the game your competitors are.

Studying our competition is how Jamie and I took over the companies of our competitors when the economy started to take down telecom organizations. A few other things played into it, but it started with acknowledging and studying who our competitors were in the first place. We didn't look over any company and decide, "We can't list them as a competitor because we are not as established as they are." We wrote down how our products were the same as theirs and how they were different. We listed the advantages that we had over our competitors. We understood our outline: who is doing what and why they were doing it better or worse. In the telecom industry, we compete against many companies and run across each other all the time. The key is to find a niche in the market.

Collect as much information as you can on your competitors, and then get to work. There isn't an industry out there that doesn't have competition. If you think you have no competition, take the time to look at your business from a different perspective. Yes, the product may be state-of-the-art, but the way you offer and promote it to the public will trace the billing model of businesses that came before you. If you think your business doesn't have competition, you may be offering a product that no one wants.

Analyze Your Competitor's Markets

What if your competitor pursues the same customers as you? If they are Fiat and you are the Volkswagen Group, you may cross paths when trying to sell your VW Beetle because Fiat is known for its compact cars. Customers who buy this vehicle are looking for a certain price tag as well as a certain functionality. It will be your job to know why Fiat is selling more cars than VW.

Take the time to model what works for your customers. If you are in the same business, your customers will expect similarities in service and approach. Don't be afraid to emulate the successes of your competitors, especially if they are doing some portion of the business better than you. Learn from your competitors' shortcomings; they are doing the same business as you and are probably doing some things wrong. Watch what they are doing in order to succeed where they fall short.

Know Your Rivals

Lastly, I want to say that keeping an eye on your competitors is not about copying their ideas. Rather, it's about getting into the mind of your rivals. Asking yourself about their strategy will help you figure out why they do the things they do, why they are successful, and why they make decisions that you wouldn't otherwise think to make. I knew who my rivals were when I stepped onto an unfamiliar call floor to coach salespeople. I wasn't threatened, though. In fact, I did all that I could to be cordial and friendly with other salespeople. The business world is sometimes so small that if you spend your time glaring at people, you will soon back yourself into a corner.

For Jamie and I, it was an intentional piece of our everyday work lives to treat our competitors with respect. It often happened that we would be standing amongst clients, before or after a sales pitch, and someone from the group would ponder aloud, "What do you think of so-and-so?"

In those moments, just like every other critical thinker, what I wanted to say was, "So-and-so has a laundry list of faults, and this is how we do things better." But my better self knew that's not how business gets done. Firstly, I would be demeaning my work to cut a competitor off at the knees. By slandering so-and-so, I've put my personal thoughts out there as fact, and in time, I could be sure that those words would come back to haunt me. Instead, my reply would be something like, "I can't speak for their work, but I can say that Terremark is successful because of these three factors."

I respect my competition. When the day comes for me to buy out my competitors, I will have made no enemies. In fact, there are hundreds of salespeople I admired and with whom I enjoyed brief working experiences who worked for our competitors. Eventually, Jamie and I were able to invite these people to be a part of our team.

Instead of spending time focusing on your rivals with the intent of taking them down, focus on your own skills. Use your emotional intelligence to position yourself. Use your relational intelligence to build the business and your networks.

Mergers and Acquisitions

Knowing what is happening in terms of mergers and acquisitions (M&A) within the market is critical to navigating major shifts in your business and competition. Never before in my life have I seen a surge of mergers happen the way they are happening today. Hundreds of telecom companies have merged or are in the process of merging. The same phenomenon is occurring within the airline industry. Twenty and even ten years ago, there was fierce competition between American airline companies. Today, there are a few stable companies that have done the work of merging with their competition to make global conglomerate companies. In the 1970s and 1980s, it was rare to hear anyone talk of one company buying another company.

My students often ask, "Why is this happening?"

My answer is that mergers are a result of a very dynamic global economy. This is what happens when you take your company global. The Internet has done wonders for shrinking our markets. Now, companies are not just competing with those in their state, region, or nation—they are competing with global markets in Brazil, Germany, China, and so on. A business that is not successful in Europe may be wildly successful in Japan. Personally, I think this is a good thing. It makes good products available all over the globe and can only benefit the growth of the economic environment.

Take a look at Fiat and Chrysler, for example. Ten years ago, Americans had no idea who Fiat was. Those select Americans who traveled could identify Fiat as a little car from Rome, Italy, but this wasn't common knowledge. Now that Chrysler has taken in Fiat, the car has become a household name. Fiat alone served Europe and South America. Now with their new product and partnership, they are serving Asia as well. It's great for the consumer because they have more of a choice. It also positively impacts the economy because the company has a new vertical where it can foster continuous growth and market its business. Prior to the merger, the CFO couldn't see profits ever coming from Beijing, but now they have a plant in the Hunan province and as of 2013, started rolling out the production of cars.

In my book, mergers and acquisitions are good, but they do come with some hard decisions to make. One of these may be the termination of employees. If you buy a company, you may have two executive assistants doing the same job. One will typically have to be let go or get transferred within the company. In the Fiat example, however, the companies were able to create more jobs by starting a brand-new market in China.

While M&A does have its negative side, I think the good far outweighs the bad. I predict many more mergers to come. Verizon bought Terremark, and within a four-year period beginning in 2011, the company turned around with the intent of selling it for much more money. It's a good thing, and it makes life easier for the consumer.

The biggest danger—largely prevented by current federal regulations—is the prospect of monopolies. In 2014, Comcast was set to merge with Time Warner Cable. The merger was approved by Comcast shareholders as well as Time Warner shareholders. Their next step was to ask the Federal Communications Commission (FCC) for approval. Both the FCC and the United States Department of Justice (DOJ) would need to approve the merger, but that didn't happened.

Seeing the monopoly coming, groups of activists banded together to alert the public, the FCC, and the DOJ of their reservations about the merger. The public was unwilling to put that much power in the hands of a single company. The newly formed organization would be offering Internet and cable services to two-thirds of the country's homes. To make it worse, Comcast readily confirmed that prices would go up. That kind of merger wouldn't help the economy; it would hinder it. The merger never happened, but consumer concern continues thanks to a growing political campaign. In the past few years, four or five companies also tried to buy T-Mobile, only to be stopped dead in their tracks by the FCC. A monopoly results in prices for the consumer going up.

As long as acquisitions and mergers are being monitored by the government, I think they make sense for business and our global economy. M&A create movement and competition in the global economy and more choice for the consumer. All in all, the market is a vast ocean with constant movement underneath. If you are the business floating above, oblivious to the life churning under the surface, then you are surely going to sink. In order to succeed in today's market, you have to be willing to make a foray into our mass global markets.

Once you identify who your competitors are and learn to treat them with respect, you will have a better chance of becoming a successful business. Think of it this way: either you will be bought out by a bigger business or your business could be the bigger fish swallowing the smaller competition. I love the market today. There is always opportunity looming in the distance. Find it and go for it!

CHAPTER 15

Parting Wisdom

There are a number of lessons I hope you have learned by looking over the adventures of my life's work. Who knows, maybe this book will change the way you do business and therefore change you. Maybe it will give you the confidence to succeed at something you previously felt uneasy about pursuing. Whatever it may be, take this moment to read my final words, because it is in the ending that the beginning really makes the most sense.

I hope you have learned that there is nothing more important than the face-to-face meeting. The anecdote about Frank Demmer throwing people's items out the window if they weren't beating the pavement for sales is in fact a true story. If I could leave you with a few final words about sales, it would be these:

1. Nothing is worth pursuing unless you are passionate about it and can deliver it with all of your energy.
2. A focus on winning is built on innovative thinking and the ability to seek out and utilize constructive criticism.
3. Nothing is gained by sitting behind your desk; you have to step into the world and make yourself known.

My biggest fear is that you will walk away without truly understanding how important it is to make a human connection with the people you are serving. Have I stressed it enough? If after reading this book—the stories of my international travels to 128 countries and successes around the globe—you are still sitting behind your desk, then please use this book to even out the legs of your toppling desk chair or nightstand, because either this information doesn't apply to you or you are not passionate about sales.

You build a business for two reasons: to create a legacy or an exit strategy. Either you want to build something great that will have a lasting impact on the world for some time to come, or you want to create something you can sell for a quick paycheck. The ones who care about the legacy never care about the money. They care about creating the brand, creating the business. As an example, I think Facebook's Mark Zuckerberg was never concerned with being a billionaire. From the very beginning, it appeared he cared about the website being up and running around the clock. He cared about his brand, which was simply his work. He was passionate about creating a social network. He didn't know that he would become a billionaire later. The passion was there.

Step into the office and make the business yours. It doesn't matter what your passion is. If anything, I hope this book has inspired you to go after what really gets you out of bed in the morning. For me, it was sales, but I know that can't be everyone's cup of tea. Not everyone is a salesperson or needs to be part of an executive team. You need to be passionate about whatever you set your mind and hands to. For instance, if you love being a nurse and are passionate about it, you should do that. However, this doesn't mean that people's interests, passions, and innate abilities don't change over time.

What comes naturally to me now is lecturing. I love talking about my experiences so much that I can get lost in a lecture in front of a room full of students. If you don't stop me, I could look up five hours later and still have things to present.

I believe that in order to be successful, you can't chase the amenities you want to have in your life: a big paycheck, fancy toys, and so on. What you do need to chase is your passion, and all the other things will fall into place—as long as you always move forward.

ABOUT THE AUTHOR

Mr. Benjamin Von Seeger is a senior sales executive known for delivering and sustaining revenue and profit gain within a competitive global telecommunications market. He built world-class sales teams and implemented proven sales processes to exponentially increase revenue for multiple wholesale telecommunications providers.

Throughout his seventeen-year career, Benjamin Von Seeger has held key sales positions with wholesale telecommunication and colocation service providers such as CENX, FiberNet Telecom Group, Terremark Worldwide—NAP of the Americas, MCI, and Mannesmann Telecommunications in Germany.

Prior to joining DELUXE—Hostopia, Benjamin Von Seeger was director of global markets with CENX, the first carried of Ethernet exchange. FiberNet/Zayo Bandwidth provides comprehensive broadband interconnectivity for the exchange of traffic, for and between multiple IP-centric and TDM-based networks. With FiberNet/Zayo Bandwidth, Benjamin Von Seeger was responsible for the development and management of millions of dollars in revenue from several international carrier accounts, such as Brazil Telecom, T Systems, France Telecom, Telefonica, and Telecom Italia.

With Terremark Worldwide—NAP of the Americas, Benjamin Von Seeger served as a vice president, where he secured millions of dollars in contracts from the largest national and international telecommunication carriers, content providers, and other major corporations from Latin America, Europe, Asia, and the United States. Terremark Worldwide, Inc. (AMEX:TMRK) was a leading operator of integrated Tier-1 Network Access Points (NAPs) and a best-in-class network services, creating technology marketplaces in strategic global locations. Terremark, a colocation and cloud-hosting provider, was sold to Verizon for $1.4 billion; Verizon paid $19 in cash for each Terremark share—about a 35 percent premium to the stock's closing price of $14.05 a share.

Benjamin Von Seeger is multilingual, with proficiency in five languages: English, Italian, Romanian, German, and Spanish. He holds a degree in business administration and international relations from Ludwig Maximilian University Munich, in Germany, and has been awarded many professional degrees and certificates. He is currently attending the Advance Management Program for business administration and management at Harvard Business School.

Ben has also served as a visiting colecturer at Keller Graduate School of Management/Devry University, enhancing the critical thinking and learning processes of undergraduate- and graduate-level students. He also served as a distinguished panelist for the graduate-level capstone projects during end-of-term evaluations. Ben continues to support the academic endeavors of students for different universities in the United States and around the world.

Open Book Editions
A Berrett-Koehler Partner

Open Book Editions is a joint venture between Berrett-Koehler Publishers and Author Solutions, the market leader in self-publishing. There are many more aspiring authors who share Berrett-Koehler's mission than we can sustainably publish. To serve these authors, Open Book Editions offers a comprehensive self-publishing opportunity.

A Shared Mission

Open Book Editions welcomes authors who share the Berrett-Koehler mission—Creating a World That Works for All. We believe that to truly create a better world, action is needed at all levels—individual, organizational, and societal. At the individual level, our publications help people align their lives with their values and with their aspirations for a better world. At the organizational level, we promote progressive leadership and management practices, socially responsible approaches to business, and humane and effective organizations. At the societal level, we publish content that advances social and economic justice, shared prosperity, sustainability, and new solutions to national and global issues.

Open Book Editions represents a new way to further the BK mission and expand our community. We look forward to helping more authors challenge conventional thinking, introduce new ideas, and foster positive change.

For more information, see the Open Book Editions website:
http://www.iuniverse.com/Packages/OpenBookEditions.aspx

Join the BK Community! See exclusive author videos, join discussion groups, find out about upcoming events, read author blogs, and much more! http://bkcommunity.com/